Timeless Bounty

*Food and Wine
in New York's
Finger Lakes*

View of Keuka Lake. *Photo courtesy Olga Bogatyrenko / Shutterstock*

TIMELESS BOUNTY

Food and Wine in New York's Finger Lakes

THOMAS PELLECHIA

Burford Books

Printed in the United States of America.

10   9   8   7   6   5   4   3   2   1

Library of Congress Cataloging-in-Publication Data

Pellechia, Thomas, author.
   Timeless bounty : food and wine in New York's Finger Lakes / Thomas Pellechia.
        pages cm
   Includes bibliographical references and index.
   ISBN 978-1-58080-175-1
   1. Agriculture--New York (State)--Finger Lakes. 2. Food--New York (State)--Finger Lakes. 3. Viticulture--New York (State)--Finger Lakes. 4. Finger Lakes (N.Y.)--History. I. Title.

   S451.N56P55 2014
   630.9747--dc23   2014015312

Halftitle: Farmland near Keuka Lake. *Courtesy Chris Houston.*

CONTENTS

The Dawn of the Finger Lakes

THE GRAIN BELT or Breadbasket of the United States reaches east from the Rocky Mountains to the Great Lakes and south to the Texas Panhandle. The rest of the country's food basket is a Pacific Coast phenomenon, specifically California, and more specifically that state's vast San Joaquin Valley, which boastfully calls itself the Food Basket of the World. It wasn't always this way.

It's easy to forget that the vast United States of America began as thirteen small colonies situated in the North and Southeast, an area that today makes up less than one-quarter of the country's landmass; the region west of the Great Lakes wasn't incorporated into the expanding republic until the mid- to late-nineteenth century. Certainly, some brave souls were pioneering before the American Revolution, but the traffic heated up after the battles had stopped, the Constitution was signed, and the new country sought to expand.

After the Revolution, local agrarian self-sufficiency prevailed and then gave way to industrial might. Enterprising citizens with talent had the opportunity to identify and meet the "daily bread" needs of a dynamic young nation with an exploding population. To house and feed the new America required expansive runs of standing hardwood, naturally fertile land that could be converted into organized farming, and acres of flowing waters for agriculture and for commerce. Few areas of the Northeast were as beautifully endowed with these combined attributes as that section of the original colonies that became New York State—and so, for almost a century after the American Revolution, New York was arguably the country's food (and drink) basket.

Fall panorama, Canandaigua Lake. *Courtesy VisitFingerLakes.com*

Today, New York State measures nearly 3,800,000 square miles. A recent New York Agriculture and Markets survey uncovered more than thirty-six thousand, mostly small farms operating in the state, generating about $4.5 billion annually. According to the survey, milk and cheese production account for half the state's farm revenue, making New York the third largest milk-producing state as well as the fourth largest cheese-producing state in the country. That's not all: New York is second in the nation in its largest fruit crop—apples. The state ranks second in wine production, as well as second in maple syrup and cabbage; it is third in overall grape production, and fourth in tart cherries, pears, sweet corn, and pumpkins.

An apple orchard in Ontario County, NY. Apples are New York State's largest fruit crop. *Courtesy VisitFingerLakes.com.*

A large share of New York's farm products are grown within a space of nine thousand square miles, in one of the most strikingly beautiful regions on the American landscape. Lush deciduous and evergreen tree-topped hills overlook vast expanses of verdant pastures that gently slope toward fecund valleys down to the shorelines of the eleven pristine oblong lakes that give the region its name: the Finger Lakes.

The Finger Lakes region of Central and Western New York was the nation's farm belt for about a hundred years after the American Revolution. Its bounty dates to the first known human beings on the North American continent, but the full story begins four hundred million years ago, before humans arrived. At that time, the area that is today the Northeast region of the United States and Canada was a vast ocean. That body of water slowly oscillated for eons, dumping successive waves of sediments and deposits taken in from the uplands to the ocean's east. Evidence of this prehistoric oceanic time is found in the marine fossils embedded in rocks that still litter New York.

This vast ocean was slow to retreat. As it drained mostly to the north and west, the ocean's forceful directional pull cut the rising surface of Central New York into a series of valleys surrounded by mountains along its northeastern region, with short hill formations—known as drumlins—still scattered about today. About 115,000 years ago, glaciers advanced from the highlands of Labrador in what is today eastern Canada. These ice rivers filled first the Central New York valleys and then rose up the drumlin-laden slopes. For the next hundred thousand years, the glaciers advanced and retreated a few times as the climate cooled and warmed. Some valleys that paralleled the advancing ice were secondarily eroded,

A corn maze in Trumansburg, New York, depicting the Finger Lakes and some of the region's popular activities. *Courtesy Chris Houston* creating "side valleys" high above the main valleys. The moving glaciers also displaced sediment in meltwater that accumulated in the valleys and flowed (often northerly) as large streams.

The last of the advancing-glacier periods took place between twenty-two and twenty-three thousand years ago across the midwestern and northeastern regions of the United States. This era is called the Wisconsin Glaciation Period, for its identified geologic location north of the Ohio River. At this time, the northern parts of the United States and Canada were completely covered with ice, while the area that is today Alaska was arid and mostly ice-free. About twelve thousand years ago, the glaciers began to retreat once more. They left behind many lakes, four of which were quite large and later named by geologists Algonquin, Warren, Tonawanda, and Iroquois. These four glacial lakes were connected by way of naturally formed outlets, which gave way to reduced water levels and rising landmass—changes that created the five Great Lakes. Algonquin Lake was separated into three lakes: Superior, Michigan, and Huron; Warren Lake became smaller and is known today as Lake Erie; the shallow Tonawanda Lake vanished into what is today the Niagara River. Sitting between receding ice on its north shore and rock deposits on its south shore, with its own outlet that flowed through New York's Mohawk Valley and to the Hudson River, Iroquois became the fifth Great Lake, Ontario. Today, Lake Ontario stretches about 125 miles west from Central New York, ending in the southern part of Canada.

Lake Ontario's southern shore is the end of a vast and uniform slope that begins at a plateau south along New York's border with Pennsylvania; most of the drumlins are situated within this expanse. Between these short hills is a system of muck hollows that meander through the region, the result of rivers left behind as the glaciers receded. Some of the rivers were plugged by sediment, ultimately carving south of Lake Ontario the eleven elongated Finger Lakes. From east to west, they are Otisco, Skaneateles, Owasco, Cayuga, Seneca, Keuka, Canandaigua, Honeoye, Canadice, Hemlock, and Conesus. The lakes are large now, but are smaller than when they first formed. For instance, Seneca Lake, thirty-eight miles long with a maximum depth of over six hundred feet, spanning almost forty-three thousand acres, once was nearly double its perimeter with a maximum depth of almost a thousand feet.

The Finger Lakes,
as seen from the
Space Station.
Photo courtesy NASA.

In a previously glaciated area, rocks and soil aren't necessarily related; that's because the rocks are dredged up locally but the soil is swept in from far and near by movements of melting ice. Just south of Lake Ontario, gray and red shale is intertwined with red sandstone, substances suitable for brick and building material like cobblestone. Across the plateau plains along the southern shores of Lake Ontario, and in the slope going south, many deep glacial deposits contain fieldstones of lime. Among this limestone is shale as well as sandstone. One of the more famous shale deposits in New York is the Salina Shale around Syracuse, still a prime source of salt. The limestone of the region exerts a major influence on crop production; its alkalinity (high pH) helps to balance the largely thin and acidic soils along the slopes and at the tops of hills.

In the plateaus and valleys, the soil is thick and runs from yellow-brown to red or pink colors; this is identified as the Ontario Soil Series. In the lowlands, glaciers deposited levels of clay, silt, and even sand and gravel in what is known as the Dunkirk Soil Series. Over the centuries, ponds and lakes were formed in these lowlands, leaving behind mud and marsh, not to mention a thriving plant life. Today, thanks to the climate-moderating effects of the lakes as well as its lower elevation, the region south of Lake Ontario, with its Ontario and Dunkirk soils, remains among the best and most fertile agricultural sections of New York State. Crops sensitive to acid, like clover and alfalfa, thrive here. The soil also supports cabbage, beans, and a variety of fruits and vegetables, as well as livestock production. West of the Ontario and Dunkirk soils are the Honeoye and Clyde soils. Honeoye is concentrated with limestone outcroppings with a mix of shallow, stony, and sandy loam. The bluegrass of Honeoye is good for growing hops, as it is on the southeastern edge of the Ontario Soil Series. The Clyde soil is largely swampy lowland with near-black material suitable for grains, hay, and a number of herbs and vegetables.

Raining "Cats and Dogs"

Because it is predominantly a hollow, the Finger Lakes region is subjected to secondary storms that generally sweep in from the Great Lakes region of the Midwest. Destructive downpours are common during the growing season. The region's slopes serve as a natural drainage system, but flooding in the flat southernmost plateau valley areas is a frequent occurrence. Next to flooding, the most striking influence that water has on Central New York is the lake-influenced tempering of late-spring and early-autumn frosts. Water changes temperature at a much slower speed than does air. The temperature of Lake Ontario can be up to fifteen degrees Fahrenheit warmer in winter and cooler in summer than adjacent land. That is good for fruit crops, especially when married with cool nights throughout the growing season. The water's effect is replicated in the interior, especially among the four largest of the eleven Finger Lakes: Cayuga, Seneca, Keuka, and Canandaigua, which combined total almost 270 perimeter miles—but the lakes do little to prevent severe frosts at the highest peaks or at the lowest muck sites that surround them. The long slopes down to the lakeshores, with good air drainage and proximity to temperate air rising from the lakes, are the safest for the majority of crops, especially grapes, which are negatively affected by mold from moisture and wild air temperature swings.

The Inhabitants

The Wisconsin Glaciation Period also produced the first human colonies in the midwestern and northeastern regions of the United States. The most persistent hypothesis is that the first human beings arrived in the Northeast from Asia via a frozen land gap that is today the Bering Strait. The earliest inhabitants settled in a part of North America that was also home to mammoths, mastodons, camels, and saber-toothed cats. The reasons behind the disappearance of these animals remain largely speculation, not the least of which is that they were hunted to extinction.

The people in the Northeast after the ice receded twelve thousand years ago were members of a Paleo-Indian culture, but since theirs pre-dates Woodland pottery-making cultures, scientists don't know to what extent the earliest humans in New York were able to take advantage of the attributes of the Finger Lakes region. We do know, however, something about the people who inhabited the region almost six thousand years ago, which is when this story of Finger Lakes bounty really begins.

1

Who Owned the Land?

The land was filled with plenty, for the Great Spirit had given to them the three sustainers of life, the corn, the bean, and the squash. Flowers bloomed, birds sang, and all the earth was glad with the Red Children, for the gifts of the Great Spirit.

On one side of a hill grew the tall, waving corn, with its silk tassels and plumes. On another side, beans, with their velvety pods, climbed toward the sky. Some distance down a third slope, beautiful yellow squashes turned their faces to the sun . . .

There came a rustling through the waving leaves, and a great sigh burst from the heart of the tall stalks. The Spirit of the corn was lonely . . . every morning at sunrise, a handsome young chief was seen to come and stand on the brow of the hill. On his head were shining red plumes. Tall and strong, and splendid he stood, wrapped in the folds of his waving blanket, whose fringed tassels danced to the summer breeze.

"Che che hen! Che che hen! Some one I would marry! Some one I would marry!" the young chieftain would sing . . .

His voice reached the Squash Maiden, on the other side of the hill. The Squash Maiden drew about her a rich green blanket, into which she had woven many flaunting gold trumpet-shaped flowers. Then she ran swiftly to the young chieftain . . .

Corn Plume looked down at the Squash Maiden sitting on her blanket at his feet . . . Corn Plume was not content. He wanted a maiden who would stand by his side, not always sit at his feet.

Then Corn Plume spoke . . . "Corn Plume cannot make Squash Maiden his wife, for he is not content with her. But she shall be Corn Plume's sister, and sit in his lodge whenever she will." . . .

Hemlock Lake, one of the smaller lakes in the western
Finger Lakes region. *Photo courtesy VisitFingerLakes.com.*

The voice of Corn Plume was again heard, singing from the hilltop, "Che che hen! Che che hen." . . . His song reached the ears of the Bean Maiden . . . Her breath was sweet as the waters of the maple. She threw off her blanket of green, and purple, and white, and stretched her twining arms to him . . .

He bent his tall plumed head to her. Her arms wound round and round the young chieftain, and Corn Plume was content.

So closely were the arms of Corn Plume and the Bean Maiden entwined, so truly were they wed, that the Indians never attempted to separate them . . .

Since the Great Spirit had placed the corn, the bean, and the squash together on a hill, the Indian said they should continue to live and grow and occupy a hill together . . . And because the Spirits of the corn and the bean are as one, the Indians not only plant and grow them together, but cook and eat them together . . .

And now, when a great rustling and sighing of the corn is heard in the White man's land, the Indians often say, "'Tis the Spirit of Corn Plume, crying for his lost Bean Maiden!"

—*Stories the Iroquois Tell Their Children* by Mabel Powers (Yeh Sen Noh Wehs), American Book Company, 1917

IN 1905, New York State Museum archaeologist Arthur Parker heard of artifacts being plowed up by farmers near Lamoka Lake, a regional lake situated in the town of Tyrone in Schuyler County and between two of the Finger Lakes, Seneca and Keuka. In 1925, seventy miles away from Lamoka Lake, Parker was the director at the Rochester Museum of Arts and Sciences (today it is the Rochester Museum and Science Center). He wanted to start an excavation of about three acres in the area, and so Parker assigned William Ritchie—who would become a well-known archaeologist—to do some fieldwork at the site (Ritchie was later joined by archaeologist Harrison Follett). Because the site was active farmland, the two men had to schedule their digging to take place before spring planting or after harvest season. Quite often, farmers who found items while plowing or digging presented them to the archaeologists, who could then indicate where best to look for more artifacts.

By 1932, Ritchie announced that the findings at the Lamoka Lake site produced clear evidence of a hunter-gatherer culture in the Finger Lakes region dating back to the Archaic Period of North American prehistory, 3500 BCE.

1 cm

Three Lamoka projectile points. *Photo courtesy Wikipedia.*

In 1935, Ritchie researched an Ontario County site along Seneca Lake near Geneva, and another site the following year in Monroe County. Dr. Ritchie was already convinced that he had uncovered an Archaic Finger Lakes culture; two years of digging at the north end of Cayuga Lake, near Union Springs, confirmed his conviction. The many sites dug defined the Lamoka culture territory from Cayuga County as far west to Monroe County. More excavations followed: the New York State Museum (1958–62), and in the decades between the 1980s and 2000s, the Buffalo Museum of Science, Utica College, and Rutgers University.

Almost forty years after its discovery, the Lamoka site was registered as a National Historic Landmark. It is a narrow bench terrace with a sandy ridge on its east end. Remnants that suggest rectangular dirt-floor dwellings measuring an average two hundred square feet were uncovered alongside low-lying dark earth mixed with shell and bone material that the archaeologists believed were refuse pits and/or fire beds. Recovery at the site included adzes as well as many points for arrows that are now known as Lamoka Points, identified by their average inch-and-a-half size and quite thick base—a Lamoka Point is as much as three times longer than it is wide. The points were made from quartz, quartzite, flint, and jasper. Along with the points, archaeologists uncovered about nine thousand shards of various pottery items, stone net sinkers, and both ground stone and polished stone tools used for weaving as well as for tree chopping. The stone tools were mostly made from slate, limestone, and basalt. Pottery-like cups were produced from turtle shells; knives and fishing hooks were made from the bones of white-tailed deer, squirrels, pigeons, and even humans. The site's location suggests that the natives, now known as the Lamoka, enjoyed easy hunting, fishing, and gathering access to distant areas either on foot or by raft, floating the numerous streams and small rivers that led south to the Chemung and Susquehanna rivers. This was mainly a hunter-gatherer culture; food scraps identified at the site include deer, fish, turkey, and pigeon; the only plant food uncovered was acorns and nuts. The Lamoka prepared meals in sandstone mortars and cooked in basin hearths covered by stone slabs.

Separate from the human bones used for tools, about four thousand human skeletal remains were uncovered at the site, producing evidence of two separate well-defined cranial types. Based on techniques to fix the age of the bones, we know that the earliest villagers were tall, slender, and long-headed; the later villagers were massively strong and broad-headed. Mutilated skeletons exhumed from refuse pits and shallow graves hint that the two groups met and were enemies. The latter villagers were the winners. This stronger, more massive dominant culture of the Lamoka is believed to have been active up to a thousand years ago, and came to be known as the Algonkian, the culture that formed the basis of northeastern Native American languages.

A communal farming people had fully replaced the Lamoka culture around the year 900. William Ritchie named this group Owasco, referring to the earliest discovered site near Owasco Lake south of Syracuse. According to Ritchie, once settled, early Owasco communities were also fiercely territorial. Wars among families, clans, and, later, separate tribes established breakaway communities throughout the northeastern United States and parts of Canada in what developed into generations of sustained animosity. Although the expanding families and communities were relatively ungoverned at first, their growing social complexity dictated some form of centralized control.

Owasco Lake.
*Photo courtesy
Chris Houston.*

The major difference between the Lamoka and the Owasco had to do with their food preferences. The former predominantly ate a meat protein diet; the latter primarily ate a diet of wild and cultivated plants supplemented with meat. The Owasco lived in villages, hamlets, and camps on fertile lands either on floodplains or at slight elevation along drumlin slopes, where they started farms. Their diet centered on what came to be known as the Three Sisters: maize (corn), beans, and squash. Along with the Bering Strait route into North America, a competing hypothesis concerning Paleo-Indians and their entry into the continent has them arriving from the Southwest by way of Central America. Some scientists speculate that the Three Sisters, plus tobacco, began as southern crops and were passed to their northern brethren from relatives in Mexico and Peru. However they got to the region, the Three Sisters crops remained the foundation of sustenance for the peoples of Central New York for almost a millennium.

At about the year 1000, Central New York tribes changed their pattern from settling on their usual lowland locations—which had to be moved often to accommodate floods—to settling in the relative permanent location of hilltops that offered both drier and more spacious accommodations for planting the Three Sisters. By the twelfth century, dozens of villages blanketed the region. Village sites of the period averaging between two and three acres and hosting estimates of up to three hundred people have been uncovered near Syracuse and about seventy-two miles west at Canandaigua. Villagers lived in small oblong houses, but archaeologists in their first discoveries also found larger structures up to sixty feet long. By the end of the thirteenth century, structures had grown even larger at other sites. This identified archaeological transition in Central New York pointed to yet another culture in the region.

The Iroquois Culture

They called themselves the Onguie-Honwe, the People of the Longhouse, referring to eighty-foot compartmentalized dwellings that were constructed from pole and bark taken from the forests. In each longhouse lived a clan made up of several families. French colonists later gave this group the name Iroquois.

The Iroquois built more permanent settlements than their predecessors and they concentrated on fortress-like living, with defensible stockade structures and guard platforms rimming the longhouses. Adjacent to the community they cleared farmland plots as large as one hundred acres, mostly in the lowlands. Because their intense farming spurred both population growth and soil exhaustion, they were forced to move to new sites every few decades.

An anonymous 1664 engraving of two Iroquois women grinding corn.
Photo courtesy Wikipedia.

From evidence at a site dated to 1400 that was uncovered in Onondaga County, near Syracuse, archaeologists believe that it was the location of two separate Iroquois villages, one larger than the other, but in unusually close proximity, signaling apparent peaceful coexistence. Then, sometime around the middle of the fifteenth century, approximately ten thousand Iroquois joined to make up a League of Five Nations that comprised the Seneca, Cayuga, Onondaga, Oneida, and Mohawk tribes. The confederacy established a common bond among the nations, yet each remained an individual self-governing community. Spanning hundreds of miles, the communities included the Mohawk Valley's site at Indian Castle, Central New York's Onondaga Castle outside Syracuse, and Seneca Castle west of Geneva (the seventeenth-century Dutch referred to the natives' longhouses at these original sites as "castles"). The five-nation communities went as far west as to Genesee Valley locations at Honeoye Falls, Geneseo, and Mount Morris. It's believed that the Iroquois confederation later served as a model for establishing the Republic of the United States of America.

For the next couple of hundred years, the Iroquois of Western and Central New York, and in the Mohawk Valley, lived in relative peace among themselves, but they joined restively in battle with the Algonquin nations of the Hudson Valley region, as well as with the Huron tribes of Canada. Central New York Iroquois fought with and defeated other Iroquois to their west, into the Great Lakes region of the Midwest, but they never managed to defeat the Algonquin to their east. Some archaeologists believe that the agricultural talent that made the Iroquois powerful turned out to be the very thing that prevented them from defeating the Algonquin, as the Hudson Valley tribes learned Three Sisters farming from their enemy, giving them a well-fed and swelling population to withstand Iroquois onslaughts.

When they weren't making war, however, the Iroquois, Huron, and Algonquin farmed, hunted, fished, and expanded their communities. More important, the enemy nations engaged in trade. The Iroquois traded their agricultural crops for tobacco with the Huron and for shells and dried clams and oysters with the Algonquin who controlled the Hudson River and the bay beds along its banks. This may have been exactly what the Iroquois coveted when they sought to conquer the Hudson Valley region—there's evidence that they adored oysters.

An Indian hunter went into the forest in search of game.

The forest was so large that it would have taken three days to journey through it. All day he followed the track of the deer, but his arrows brought him no food.

At night, he came to a dark, swift-running stream. He was tired and hungry.

"Here," said he, "I will lie down and rest until sunrise" . . . The hunter ran along the stream. It was very dark. He felt no soft pine needles under his moccasined feet, only the knotted roots of trees.

Suddenly the great roots of an oak tree reached out and caught him. He could not free his foot from the oak's grasp . . .

It was now two days since he had tasted food . . . Three times did the sun again rise and set, yet the tree did not let go its hold . . .

As the sun rose on the fifth day, a bird flew into the tree. He saw the hunter lying on the ground . . . The bird asked the hunter what he could do for him, and the hunter whispered, "You are strong. You can fly a long trail. Go and tell the chief of my people."

The bird flew swiftly away with the message . . . The West Wind tried to blow him back. A black cloud came up to frighten him, but he went through it . . . Straight to the wigwam of the chief, he carried his message . . .

The chief had called together the young men who were fleet of foot, and was about to send them forth to find the lost hunter . . . a beautiful dove-colored bird had flown close to his ear and had spoken to him in soft, low tones . . . The chief told the young men what the bird had said, and they set off on the trail the bird had named. Before sunset, they had found the lost hunter.

Carefully they freed him from the grasp of the great oak and bore him to his people. That night there was a feast and a dance in his honor. Ever since, the Indians have loved the birds that carry the messages, and they never shoot a pigeon.

—*Stories the Iroquois Tell Their Children* by Mabel Powers (Yeh Sen Noh Wehs), American Book Company, 1917

Though the Iroquois were expansionists, they were also content with their New York surroundings. They had fertile lowlands and gentle slopes on which to grow the Three Sisters and other crops like hemp for twine to make nets; they had myriad rivers and streams on which to float their canoes, which took them to large lakes where fish were plentiful; and they had the forests. The hills of Central New York were dense with trees. When they needed wood, they used axes and fire to clear and remove just enough trees to accomplish their task, whether it was for heat in winter, for cooking, or to build longhouses and communities. The forests also provided deer meat and skins for curing, pelts for clothing, and nuts to come raining down on them. When they weren't canoeing, and since they did not have horses, the Iroquois traveled on foot. In fact, they did most of their gardening work manually, without much help from animals.

Photo courtesy
VisitFingerLakes.com.

Iroquois squashes were mainly the summer variety. There were many different types, predominant among them the field pumpkin, the crooked yellow squash, and the bush summer squash. They also grew a number of varieties of gourds to make cooking bowls, dining utensils, plates, cups, ornaments, and receptacles used in ritual ceremonies.

In midsummer, they ate the plentiful squash crops, but they had to wait until late summer and autumn to harvest corn and beans. Later still, they harvested winter squash.

Their maize was not as sweet as the hybrid corn of today; it was either white dent (named for the indentation at the top of its kernel) or white flint (white corn intermingled with colored kernels; it was as hard as flint). At harvesttime, many corn ears were roasted in a row over a fire until the kernels were dry and then they were shelled and dried again, in the sun. With their moisture removed,

Canandaigua Lake.
*Photo courtesy
Chris Houston.*

the kernels were lighter in weight, making it easier to carry the food over long distances on hunts or in battle with the Algonquin. Mixed with maple sap, stored dried corn also produced a nutritious meal in times of famine brought on by temporary unfavorable weather conditions. As the autumn progressed into winter, the natives turned some maize into hominy by soaking kernels in lye; they also turned some to meal by pounding it in a stone or wooden mortar. The legendary Iroquois leader and co-founder of the five-nation confederation, Hiawatha, referred to eating "yellow cakes"—unleavened baked cornmeal bread. They also ate cornmeal mush mixed with meat and seed oils.

There were no dairy products in an Iroquois settlement; the bean was second to meat as an important nitrogenous food. Beans were of the climbing, kidney bean type, which could survive on poorer soil than maize. The Iroquois dropped bean seeds among the corn plants, allowing the beans to symbiotically cling and grow up the cornstalks. They often fed on boiled maize and beans pressed with oils from fish or sunflower seeds, and beans cooked slowly with corn in a dish that resembled what we know today as succotash.

An Old Family Recipe for Succotash

Ingredients

1 cup cooked lima or kidney beans

½ cup whipped, unsalted butter, divided

¼ teaspoon salt

2 tomatoes, peeled and chopped

2 teaspoons maple syrup

2 ears corn kernels, fresh from the cob

Directions

1. Add the beans to a saucepan with ¼ cup of the butter and the salt; mix and warm them.

2. In a second saucepan, heat the tomatoes on medium; mix in the syrup and the rest of the butter. Cook for about 20 minutes, or until tender.

3. Stir the beans and the corn into the tomatoes and cook for 10 minutes on medium heat.

Serves 4

Harvest was followed with a festival of thanksgiving; there were about six festivals each year, one after each harvest. After all the harvesting, a quantity of corn was dried for winter storage in cribs. After allowing them to dry out, the Iroquois stored beans, nuts, tubers, and hard grain seeds in underground storage pits. Meats were dried and smoked for storage, and sometimes frozen. Meat was also mixed with berries and deer tallow to make a high-protein preserve for a kind of meat jerky called pemmican.

The Iroquois tapped forest maple trees for sweetener and to make beer. Wild grapes also flourished. The natives ate them and cooked with them, but no record of cultivated grapevines or organized grape fermentation has surfaced.

The shores of Cayuga and Seneca lakes where Iroquois sites have been identified were once lined with the Kentucky coffee tree—*Gymnocladus canadensis*. The tribes used the raw beans to make rattles, and since the raw beans are poisonous, they learned to roast the beans to make a brew. Other plants the Central New York Iroquois cultivated included leek, Jerusalem artichoke, arum, chestnut, sassafras, and wintergreen. Their heavy reliance on farming at some point forced the Iroquois to design cultivating, harvesting, and storing implements and devices to make the hard work easier. Agriculturally based innovations passed down from them include interplanting pumpkin, corn, and beans, hoeing and hilling for weed control, the husking peg, scarecrows to keep birds at bay, and the corncrib airing device.

Until the European settlers introduced invasive species to the New World, pests were not a major farm problem for the Iroquois, but Central New York had and has a moist climate in summer, which meant that insects and disease did strike at times. The only defense against pests and disease that the Iroquois employed was either the medicine man or the practice of women disrobing in the dark and spreading their garments over the planted crop boundaries, about which Henry Wadsworth Longfellow wrote the following poem.

In the night when all is silence,
In the night when all is darkness,
When the Spirit of Sleep, Nepahwin,
Shuts the doors of all the wigwams,
So that not an ear can hear you,
So that not an eye can see you,
Rise up from your bed in silence,
Lay aside your garments wholly.
Walk around the fields you planted,
Round the borders of the cornfields,
Covered by your trees only,
Robed with darkness as a garment,
Thus the fields shall be more fruitful,
And the passing of your footsteps
Draw a magic circle around them,
So that neither blight nor mildew,
Neither burrowing worm nor insect,
Shall pass o'er the magic circle,
Not the dragon-fly, Kno-ne-she,
Nor the spider, Subbekashe,
Nor the grasshopper, Pah-puk-keena,
Nor the mighty caterpillar,
Way-muk-kwana, with the bear-skin,
King of all the caterpillars!

The Kentucky coffee tree was used by the Iroquois in the Finger Lakes region.
Photo courtesy Wikipedia.

Pumpkins,
Ontario County.
*Photo courtesy
VisitFingerLakes.com.*

Perhaps the garment-spreading ritual is an Iroquois agricultural innovation to control weeds and ground pests that present-day gardeners recognize when they lay down black plastic.

The Iroquois loved fruit, too. Among their favorites was the small deciduous black plum tree—*Prunus nigra*—native to the Northeast. They dried the plums in lye and ate them throughout the winter. They also had access to a willow herb—*Epilobium ciliatum*—until the plants were overtaken in the wild by the more virulent spreading of black and red bramble fruit bushes. According to *A History of Agriculture in the State of New York* by U.P. Hedrick, an early-twentieth-century head of Cornell University's Agricultural Experiment Station in Geneva, Central New York tribes relied on a couple hundred separate fruit species; with the black plums they ate blueberries, cranberries, dewberries, gooseberries, huckleberries, raspberries, and of course grapes. They also enjoyed the fruit of the deciduous wild pin cherry tree, which must have loved potash, as the plant grew rapidly after a burn clearing. The Geneva Experiment Station grounds today include the site of a once extensive Iroquois fruit orchard.

The same author called horticulture "an elegant branch of husbandry," pointing out that humans planted vegetables, fruits, and flowers only after reaching an advanced stage of civilization. Surely, their environment gave the Iroquois a great deal with which to work, and as their population swelled they certainly learned to cultivate many of the plants that they had relied on in the wild. In the process of engaging in their elegant branch of husbandry, they also began ever so slowly the process of changing Central New York's environment.

The White Man Comes

The natives had been changing forests slowly, but the task of clearing the woodlands was set in motion after the arrival of foreigners who docked along the North American coastline. Successful forays into South and North America by explorers from powerful European empires planted and cultivated in the seventeenth century something completely new to New York: colonial settlements.

At first, the vast forests that ran east to west throughout the Great Lakes regions saw to it that the Iroquois retained ownership of their land. Central and Western New York remained an exotic subject among colonists along the Hudson as trappers and traders ventured west and came back—if they came back—with stories of lakes, rivers, salt streams, forests, wolves, and fierce "savages." Over time, colonial interest turned into a dream to tame the wild. When settlers did finally act on that dream, success was difficult yet possible. The Dutch and the French were the first Europeans to focus on the forests—and the British weren't far behind. The volume of trees for settlers to take down with their primitive tools was daunting, as was the specter of facing those wolves, large cats, bears, and "savages" who showed little inclination to let them in. It took nearly two hundred years for white settlers to fully populate the lands west of the Hudson and into the Appalachians, but populate they did—in the end at the expense of the Iroquois nations as well as many of the trees.

Ferocious animals notwithstanding, the forests fed settlers with deer, rabbit, turkey, and other game while they worked to clear the land. Streams and rivers that serpentined forest floors provided an abundance of fish. The animal meat was supplemented with a diet of wild berries and nuts of the forests. The early European settlers lived a hunter-gatherer life similar to the ancient Lamoka. They used well-trodden Lamoka-Iroquois trails as their most reliable way to make it inland from Albany or from the Mohawk Valley all the way west to the Genesee Valley and north to Lake Ontario. As they worked to clear land and build homes, the settlers' could also raise cash from the forests by selling hardwood lumber as well as the potash from burned clearings. Many made a great deal of cash in animal fur, too. The products were sent to colonial mother countries.

With the Dutch, then the British profiting from trade in New York and the French dealing mainly in pelts from Canada, the fur trade became a fiercely lucrative and competitive industry—as evidenced by the war in 1609 between the Iroquois and the French with their Huron allies. Labeled the Beaver Wars, it was fought mainly in the Mohawk Valley. Almost sixty years after the war began, three nations in the Iroquois five-nation confederacy made peace with the French, but the Mohawks were not among them. Soon enough, the French militia burned Mohawk villages—and burned their crops as well. The beaver in New York did not fare well either.

Irondequoit Bay, near the city of Rochester, with Lake Ontario in the background.
Photo courtesy Chris Houston.

The remainder of the seventeenth century saw a series of skirmishes and wars throughout the central and western regions of New York. In 1687, the French wiped out a Seneca homeland near Irondequoit Bay on the north end of the city of Rochester, along Lake Ontario's southern shoreline. The attack prompted the Iroquois confederacy to sign on with France's age-old archenemy, the British, who had set their sights firmly on the west. This alliance came to the fore later during the French and Indian War. When that war ended, the Iroquois were rewarded by a British decree that forbade settlers beyond the Appalachian Mountains to the west. The decree was unenforceable, however, forcing the Iroquois to eventually give up their interest that far west of New York.

In the early part of the eighteenth century, the five-nation confederacy was expanded to six when the Tuscarora were forced by British colonials to flee north from the Carolinas and seek the protection of their successful New York Iroquois brethren. Toward the end of the century, however, colonial uprisings in New England that had spread south and west served as a wedge through the Iroquois confederation. The Mohawk, Onondaga, Cayuga, and Seneca sided with Britain; the Oneida and Tuscarora were on the side of the colonists. Another major Mohawk Valley village and crop burning took place, in an area known as Cherry Valley, but this time the Iroquois perpetrated the conflagration against settlers. This event led to an infamous 1779 raid in the Finger Lakes region.

As one of two officers to command the Finger Lakes raid, President George Washington chose General John Sullivan. Sullivan had lost the first Continental army battle in the Revolution, which had been fought in Brooklyn a few years earlier. In that battle, the British took Sullivan prisoner and then sent him to Staten Island, where John Adams and Washington were holed up. Sullivan's task was to deliver an unsuccessful invitation to the colonials to surrender.

With his commission to raid the Finger Lakes region, Sullivan might have seen a chance to prove himself. He certainly took to heart Washington's order to "not merely overrun, but destroy" the British-Iroquois alliance in New York. Sullivan's army marched through the dense forests of New York, making its way along the southern tier of the Finger Lakes. In and around the village of Painted Post, where the Chemung River is about to meet the Cohocton River, his troops ambushed an Iroquois settlement, killing natives, ravaging their land,

and burning the valuable Three Sisters crops. The army contingent continued on the path west until reaching the Genesee Valley, killing and burning along the way not only vegetable and grain crops, but also many acres of fruit trees. Sullivan doubled back on the route to make sure to pick up any stray Iroquois or crops that might have escaped the army's wrath on its first pass. The raid was successful in that it spelled the end of Iroquois dominance in the Finger Lakes region, but it did not quite end the British-Iroquois alliance that held until the end of the thirty-two-month War of 1812 between Britain and the United States.

Revolutionary Americans expressed particular interest in the Iroquois method of encircling small man-made hills with rows in which corn and beans were planted, with squash nearby. The pattern was to switch crops within the rows from year to year in what was another Iroquois innovation: crop rotation. The rotation served to reinvigorate potentially depleted soil and to keep disease in check. Some in Sullivan's army were smart enough to save corn seed for future possibilities, compliments of the Iroquois corn storage sheds. Captain Richard Bagnall returned from the raid to Plymouth, Massachusetts, with corn seeds from a sweet variety named Papoon that he discovered at the northern end of the Susquehanna River.

The ferocity of its wars with the Iroquois kept France from establishing a stronghold in the Finger Lakes region. Among the earliest settlers in the central part of New York were the Dutch of the Holland Land Purchase Company known as Hollanders. Their main settlements were east of Syracuse, in Cazenovia and Ellicotville. A Holland Land Purchase agent, John Lincklaen, founded Cazenovia in 1793; the town was named for his boss, Theophilus Cazenove. In an area first settled in 1815, the town of Ellicotville was established in 1820 and named for Joseph Ellicot, the top agent of the Holland Land Purchase Company. The businessmen representing the Dutch were not exactly schooled in agriculture; neither were the settlers who followed them, whether Dutch or British, who came later. In a settlement at Cattaraugus to the west of Syracuse, Holland Company land agent Jacob Otto pioneered the practice of accepting crops as payment for land, but the crops weren't always valuable, not until settlers embraced Iroquois agricultural innovations —in turn, the Iroquois learned about the horse and of the utility of the oxen. More important, each learned of crops that were new to the group—the orchard that the Iroquois operated on what is now part of Cornell University's Agricultural Experiment Station at Geneva included an apple orchard, a crop that the Iroquois didn't cultivate until European settlers introduced the eating apple to Central New York.

Neither Iroquois nor early European settlers were large-scale farmers. What they grew, they grew to sustain the family or the clan. For settlers, raising livestock was haphazard. Cattle were left to roam the natural pastures of the forest in the hope that they'd find enough food for survival. Thin and scrawny from having to eat weeds and twigs, the ones that survived might die from eating poisons in the forests. Such weakened cattle were not to be counted on to provide enough milk or for quality butter; cheese making was hardly even considered. Attempts by settlers to raise sheep often succeeded at feeding predators instead, leaving them little in the way of wool to harvest. Hogs were important to early settlers, but even they didn't particularly fare well on the hardscrabble land.

The greatest abundance was in apples and pears, which were not yet cultivated by grafting but grown the arduous way, from seed. The apple's primary use was as cider. Colonials drank cider morning, noon, and night. Cider was also legal tender to pay for the professional services of doctors, lawyers, and haberdashers. Early settlers grew some peaches, too, many of which went into brandy, as did a greater portion of ripe pears. Sour cherries were also a favorite of the settlers, for pies. Like the Iroquois, the settlers did not know the secret to cultivating the multitude of wild bramble fruits throughout the region—that discovery came in the nineteenth century. Still, also like the Iroquois, settlers valued the tiny fruits and spent many hours at harvesttime foraging the patches of sunlight throughout the forests that brought the dark fruits to ripeness.

Believing that they all were poisonous, settlers were afraid to eat the mushrooms they found growing under large old trees in the forests. Their main plant foods were dandelion and cowslips, plus the leaves of certain trees and shrubs. In fact, Central New York settlers appear to have had no idea how to grow vegetables. They knew little about fertilizing with manure, and instead of considering the potash from burn clearings as their own fertilizing material they sold it for export to Europe. There the potassium nitrate went into making gunpowder, which made the sale of potash quite profitable. They did, however, use fish bones to fertilize their cornrows, a practice the settlers were sure to have learned from the Iroquois (fish bones were discovered among the cornrows that had been destroyed during Sullivan's campaign). Like the Iroquois, when a settler's land was used up, the settler moved his small agricultural plot to a new clearing.

Clearing is what New York seemed always to need in the eighteenth century. During the American Revolution, colonial soldiers from home as well as soldiers from across the seas often had to clear dense forests before they could even engage in battle. Still, the area had great appeal. When the war ended, many soldiers on both sides brought home stories of the beauty and promise of the vast forests of Western New York. New Englanders were especially interested as they had always been interested in New York. In a convoluted and involved string of decrees and proclamations, both Massachusetts and New York believed theirs was the official claim on what lay west of the Mohawk Valley. After much wrangling, a solution in 1787 gave Massachusetts official claim on much of what today constitutes the Finger Lakes/Genesee Valley regions. In 1788, Massachusetts sold its claim of the land stretching from west of Seneca Lake to the Genesee River and within the north–south boundary just south of Lake Ontario to the border with Pennsylvania. In all, 2.6 million acres went to two Massachusetts speculators, Oliver Phelps and Nathaniel Gorham.

Nathaniel Gorham, one of the two speculators who purchased in 1788 what is now most of the Finger Lakes region.
Illustration by

In the settlement with New York, Massachusetts gained the right to make a treaty with the Seneca. The property boundary covered in the land right referred to as the "pre-emption right" is today still named the Pre-Emption Line or Road; it is situated west of Seneca Lake and runs north–south through parts of Ontario, Wayne, Yates, Steuben, and Schuyler counties. Land west of the line was placed under the sovereignty of New York. The original line was to run north from the Pennsylvania border to Lake Ontario, but surveyors cutting their way through the dense forest, marking trees along the way to follow for an official set of lines to run later, used a marine compass that led them a little to the west. No one knows if it was intentional, but the mistake, plus problems with gaining rights from the Seneca, caused headaches for Phelps and Gorham. Within two years of their purchase, the two were forced to sell what remained—about 1.3 million acres—to Robert Morris, a onetime privateer during the Revolutionary War who became quite wealthy and financed the last major engagement of the war, at Yorktown. After the war, Morris had become the head of the US Treasury, a senator, and a land speculator; in that last position, he not only went broke but also went to debtor's prison. In 1797, Morris's agent sold the land to three Englishmen: William Hornby, Patrick Colquhoun, and Sir William Pulteney. (Pulteney was married to the niece to the Earl of

Seneca Lake.
*Photo courtesy
Chris Houston.*

Bath, England.) The three sent a Scot named Charles Williamson to act as agent for what came to be known as the Pulteney Estate. Williamson was a captain in the British army during the American Revolution. He was sent to New England toward the latter part of the war, was taken prisoner in Boston, and never saw a battle. What he did see in the New World, though, he liked. Not being an American citizens and unable to manage held land from abroad, the Pulteney Estate owners sent the eager Williamson to become a naturalized American citizen and represent their interests by settling their land.

Guy J. McMasters told the rousing story of the Pulteney Estate settlement in his wordy 1853 account, *The History of the Settlement of Steuben County*. McMasters was the son of Scots who had fled religious persecution to Ireland, where Guy was born. In 1790, at age twenty, McMasters set out for America with a few suits, some shirts, and a chest of carpenter's tools. He landed in Baltimore and got a job as a journeyman carpenter. A year later, on a visit with relatives west of Baltimore, he saw a newspaper ad that attracted him to Northumberland, Pennsylvania. The ad called for mechanics and laborers seeking good wages to help a Captain Charles Williamson build a new community in a new territory in New York. Being of Scottish parents, McMasters obtained from the Scot Williamson a well-paid job as foreman of construction crews assigned to erect towns and villages. In 1795, with a lot of money saved, he gave up the construction business to become a merchant servicing the growing settlements. Along with financial rewards, McMasters held many offices over the years, including sheriff, justice of the peace, judge, and postmaster; he also spent three years in the New York State legislature representing a portion of the Pulteney Estate.

Throughout the first few years of the Revolutionary War, the Tioga and Cohocton valleys along the Finger Lakes' southern tier were untouched by combatants. Until Sullivan's campaign, the area was largely used as a passageway, especially for access to the Susquehanna River. When the war ended, the region was a dense wilderness that sparsely housed traders and woodsmen until the Phelps-Gorham survey established an office at what is today Painted Post, near the point where the Chemung and Cohocton rivers meet. The office was in the home of two traders, William Harris and his son.

Within a few years, ex-Revolutionary soldiers mostly from the Pennsylvania and Massachusetts regiments that took part in Sullivan's campaign had begun to settle land going west along the Cohocton, especially on the valley floors. They planted maize and other crops and planned to raise cattle, but these were no easy tasks, as the field grass was thick with unyielding roots that had to be burned rather than plowed and the grass was largely inedible to cattle. After successive burnings, field grass roots gave way to lush, tender grasses that the animals could digest; some spots were made soft enough to accommodate crops. For commerce, the new settlers traded wood and furs—whatever the surrounding forests provided—and they tended crops of maize and other grains, some of which they sent downriver to Tioga to the newly established Shepard's Mill for flouring. The forest provided them with logs to build housing and, as the community grew, to build a fortress-like fence around it. Remaining Iroquois in the region at first were antagonistic, but over time developed a trading and even social relationship with the settlers. The area became part of the Pulteney Estate.

Pulteney Estate representative Captain Williamson arrived in Baltimore in 1791. Before setting out for New York, he made a few acquaintances, people he would later lure to the Finger Lakes region. His next stop was Northumberland, Pennsylvania, at the west branch of the Susquehanna, where he set up an office. As winter approached, Williamson made his way to the Genesee region via Albany and then west through the Mohawk Valley, where he saw and mentioned in a journal the ruins of old German farms. Along the way, he encountered a few settlers here and there, until he reached Seneca Lake, where he came upon what his notes referred to was "an advanced white settlement." He moved farther west into the Genesee Valley to find himself surrounded by a vast wilderness in which his mind's eye saw settlements and commerce. By the following summer, Williamson was determined to cut a road from Northumberland to the Genesee River, which meant crossing the wild Allegheny Mountains. Luckily, within a few months he and a party of men discovered a trail that began at Williamsport in Pennsylvania and traveled northwest about 150 miles, taking them right into the Genesee region.

In 1792, Williamson's request to his bosses in Europe to send men to build a road was answered with a group of two hundred Germans made up of several families from Hamburg. Led by woodsman Benjamin

Patterson, seven Pennsylvanians and the Germans set out to open the road by way of the Tioga and Cohocton rivers in September, bringing with them cattle for milk. As city people, the Germans had never seen such wilderness. The arduous task before them was made worse by the specter of possible annihilation from encounters with bears and all manner of wild creatures. At Painted Post, some of the Germans stayed behind while the rest of them moved on with the Pennsylvanians. The German families who stayed held back one cow, and after they discovered a field of potatoes, they feasted on the first ever of that crop to be grown in the region. Patterson was later forced to pay the settler to whom the crop belonged.

It took over eight months of hacking to clear a road, but by spring the Germans and Pennsylvanians reached the outer western edge of the Pulteney Estate. Each German family was given a house and fifty acres, provisions to last a few months, farming implements, and some cattle and sheep. The Hamburg Germans were as ill equipped as any city slicker to operate farms, however. In short order, they had eaten all their livestock and, amid some of the most fertile land in North America, squandered their planting seed—as well as rebelling against Williamson. The Germans were first imprisoned and then sent to Canada. In 1795, Daniel Faulkner settled the area as the village of Dansville.

Free of the Germans, Williamson decided to go to the Genesee region himself to set up what he referred to as a new Babylon on the banks of the Cohocton. His dream was to build, out of the vast wilderness that was the Pulteney Estate, a city to rival the great cities of the world. He made his way along the path that the Germans had cut and when he arrived about sixteen miles northwest of the mouth of the Cohocton, far short of the end of the road, he was taken by what he saw. From an elevated site, Williamson looked out on a fifteen-or-so-mile stretch of pine, elm, sycamore, and an alluvial basin that led to the southern shore of a large crooked lake (Keuka Lake). This was to be his Babylon.

There was money to be made in developing Western and Central New York. Charles Williamson's dream to build a city on the hill became a stirring part of that development, one that relied on the vast stretch of timber situated south of Keuka Lake in the flat expanse that Williamson could see reaching about twelve miles north to the southern tip of the cursive-*y*-shaped lake. The valley was first referred to as Pine Plains for its pine tree density; later, after clearing, it was called the Pleasant Valley for its quiet peacefulness and steady fertility. For the coming few years, Pulteney Estate money from Britain financed Williamson's dream, which included the arrival of Revolutionary War soldiers and various Scots, British, and Irish families as settlers. First, the task was to clear the area of rattlesnakes. The reptiles flourished in the untouched forest floor; it took years to chase them completely into the mountains.

Beginning in 1793, on that little hill that he loved, with McMasters as foreman, Williamson set about to establish the village of Bath. He chose the name to honor the Lady of Bath, England, who was married to William Pulteney. The first business for the new village was to establish a sawmill to process logs into homes for the initial fifteen families, who arrived by the end of the year. The sawmill was a few miles west of the center of the new village, in what is today the town of Kanona. A gristmill for food, and another sawmill to accommodate the expected arrival of more and more settlers soon followed. In the spring of 1794, Williamson had an area cleared in the center of Bath that would become Pulteney Square, plus about four surrounding acres cleared for his home, a garden, and a spot to house the gardener from England that he requested and received, as well as to establish a land office. The village also received its first public house and tavern, which back then was indication of a successful community.

Williamson aimed to suck trade away from the Hudson and Mohawk regions, making Bath a commercial center by its access to the Cohocton and Chemung rivers and then on the Susquehanna as far south as Baltimore. Bath was to be his rival to New York City. That same year, Guy McMasters built an ark sixteen feet wide and seventy-five feet long, then loaded it with provisions, water, and a commercial cargo of barrels and hogshead staves worth as much as eight hundred dollars. With a crew, he set out for the Susquehanna. They made it thirty-five miles to Painted Post in six days, loaded up on more provisions, and set out on the Chemung River, which got them to the Susquehanna at Waverly, Pennsylvania. From there, it took four days to get within twenty miles of Harrisburg (about two hundred miles from Painted Post). They hit a rock and were forced to lay over for repairs. When someone at Harrisburg offered McMaster six hundred dollars plus a horse worth two hundred, the first commercial trip from Bath down the Susquehanna was aborted. Oddly, the experience gave McMasters a new passion to become a merchant; it caused Williamson to hire a Scot named Andrew Smith to supervise about thirty men to clear land for cultivation and make the rivers navigable for commerce.

Williamson worried over adding more and more settlers to his dream city, but as time went by the owners in London grew discontented. They saw little profit in the way Williamson went about his business, and they did not like the stories that came back with people who had tried venturing to Bath but could not make it there; they told of rampant land speculation and they recounted the rise of the always suspicious theater entertainment, gambling, and drinking industries. With an onslaught of new settlers plus a weather-driven famine, Williamson was forced to spend large amounts of money to bring flour and meat in from Northumberland and other locales. Ten years after his arrival, he was fired for being a costly dreamer. The Pulteney Estate investors replaced him with Robert Troup, Esquire, a New York City lawyer whose main interest in the Pulteney Estate was fiduciary. Yet between 1796 and 1800, the rivers were made navigable and a slow but steady community was built that stretched throughout the Pleasant Valley.

Corn was the first food of settlers, because growing it required only a clearing and some seeds to drop into the soil. Harvesting corn was a leisurely event that could last a month or more until the crop was all brought in. The combination of minimal preparation to plant corn and the extended harvest gave settlers a nutritious food crop that did not interrupt their busy schedule of settlement building. Corn also served to loosen the soil to better accept a rotation of wheat plantings. Settlers threw bean seeds around the corn and planted squash, just the way the Iroquois taught them. They also learned from the Iroquois how to cook these foods, how to dry the array of wild bramble fruits available to them, and where the best fishing was among the many streams, rivers, and lakes of the region.

Timber was the largest cash-producing commodity on the Pulteney Estate, followed by wheat and pork. Wheat was successful in the New World almost from the beginning of the colonies. After the soil was exhausted, and an insect blight occurred on Long Island, wheat farming moved to Central New York and into the Genesee Valley (the valley later was called the Granary of the Country). From the Pulteney Estate, thousands of bushels of wheat and hundreds of barrels of pork per year went down the Susquehanna on arks to Baltimore for trade. Guy McMasters became a successful trader and merchant, opening a store in Dansville and one in Penn Yan, a village situated at the northeast branch of Keuka Lake. Understanding the dangers in sending wheat on the three-hundred-mile journey to Baltimore, he also bought about eight hundred acres in an area of the Pleasant Valley known as Cold Springs; there he set up a flour mill as well as a sawmill. The flour mill was to send wheat to Baltimore as packaged flour, which would bring him much more money per pound. He sent out notices to wheat-farming settlers in Dansville and Penn Yan. In the first year, he bought twenty thousand bushels of wheat. As his business expanded, wheat began to come to him from as far as Seneca County to the east, Ontario County to the north, and the Genesee River valley to the west. The new Bath settlement boss, Colonel Troup, made a deal with McMasters to use the land agent office in Bath as a payment draft clearinghouse.

After McMaster's business proved profitable, his next project was to build a schooner in 1807 that carried thirty tons of cargo to make the twenty-plus miles from the southern tip of Keuka Lake to Penn Yan.

When Gorham and Phelps purchased the vast Finger Lakes and Genesee region, a wave of religious movements was sweeping across the Northeast. Jemima Wilkinson headed one of those waves after she disagreed with her Quaker religious leader in Philadelphia. Headstrong and mystical, the Vermont-born Wilkinson (a distant ancestor of actor Meryl Streep) was considered a seer by a group of a few hundred who eventually followed her to New York. They named their sect the Public Universal Friends.

Wilkinson bought from Phelps-Gorham twelve thousand acres at eighteen cents an acre. Before she took the Universal Friends to settle in Western New York in the summer of 1788 at the north end of Keuka Lake, she sent two dozen followers in 1787 to scout land for farming. With some crops established, the scouting group welcomed Wilkinson and sixty families to settle the area, which they named New Jerusalem. The Universal Friends modeled their fields of crops after the Iroquois and in fact became closely allied with them. After establishing large plantings of the Three Sisters and a few other crops, they established herds of cattle, pigs, and sheep. New Jerusalem became a draw that attracted settlers from hundreds of miles away to tap into farm supplies and farming advice. The Universal Friends' town grew rapidly. By 1790, the year of the first census, the town of New Jerusalem was the largest non-indigenous settlement in the western part of New York. That same year, a Wilkinson disciple, Richard Smith, built the first gristmill at the eastern edge of New Jerusalem, closer to Seneca Lake, in an area the Iroquois called Kashanquash and that the Universal Friends called Kashong; it became the town of Dresden in 1811. Kashong was soon filled with grain fields to supply the mill.

A successful and wealthy Pennsylvania farmer and businessman named David Wagener sold his holdings and followed Wilkinson to New York. Never truly a part of the Universal Friends and always a businessman, Wagener made another move, but not too far. He settled in 1795 at the north tip of the east branch of Keuka Lake in the area that later became the village of Penn Yan and the seat of Yates County. Wagener bought an old sawmill and one year later established a new gristmill, each at the outlet of the lake. He died in 1799 at age forty-seven, but his family stayed in the milling business.

Toward the end of the eighteenth century, the growing populations of New Jerusalem and Penn Yan were still engaged in subsistence farming, but that was soon to change. One of Wagener's sons, Abraham, ran a mill with the express purpose of servicing the local farmers who brought their buckwheat, wheat, oats, and corn for flouring. Penn Yan became a successful commercial hub, and Guy McMasters built his schooner in 1807 so that he could exploit that success.

McMasters faced an inland and seafaring mercantile embargo imposed by the federal government during the Napoleonic wars. The embargo was to prevent the British navy in a process the Crown called "impressment," and that Thomas Jefferson saw as simple piracy. Penn Yan merchants used the embargo to prevent what they viewed as a threat to their established and profitable milling businesses. McMasters's response was to build a wheat storage facility at each end of the lake and proceed with his plans, but he soon discovered that when the lake froze over in winter, he was effectively out of business for a few months. To his Penn Yan rivals' delight, McMasters lost money. Seeking another way, he trekked to Iroquois camps to make trade deals with them: wheat, flour, and pork for pelts, furs, and deer haunches (hams). In his first trade with the Seneca, despite the embargo, McMasters salted and smoked about three thousand hams, took them down the Susquehanna, and sold them in Philadelphia and Baltimore at two shillings per pound. The embargo, however, made it near impossible to continue the long journeys to Baltimore and Philadelphia without incident and loss, so he started another business at his Cold Springs mill. From local wheat, corn, and rye, McMasters produced brandy, gin, and cordials that he sold direct to settlers for as much as ten shillings per gallon. He traded the liquor with the Iroquois at the same value.

The record shows that by 1816, along with packaged flour, McMasters sold in Baltimore and Boston about one million board feet of pine and one hundred thousand board feet of cherry and curled maple, along with many barrels of distilled spirits. The local bounty made him so successful that he became a pillar of the Pulteney Estate.

2

—

Settling In

A T THE START OF THE NINETEENTH CENTURY, even with fewer trees, the woodlands of Central and Western New York were standing and in great demand. A profitable lumber economy had been established in the area south of Keuka Lake, putting natural waterpower to use at sawmills and creating an engine for further commerce. Commercial boats regularly floated the Cohocton, Chemung, and Susquehanna on their way to and from Philadelphia and Baltimore. Commerce stirred more settlements, which stirred more flour and grain mills. With or without him, Captain Charles Williamson's dream to make the Cohocton area a commercial hub to compete with the Hudson River may have been on its way toward becoming a reality, but fate had another idea.

Settlements Break Out

According to author Elmer Otterbein Fippin in his book *Rural New York,* liquor was so important that many grain millers put their best toward producing spirits and used only the second grade for flour. Fippin speculated that in the early nineteenth century, Central New York boasted more breweries and distilleries than gristmills, with stills lining the shores of the Finger Lakes, Lake Ontario, as well as smaller waterways. In the early part of the nineteenth century, the town of Geneva alone hosted thirteen stills and four gristmills. A settlement design of the period called for one gristmill, one brewery, and ten distilleries per settlement, and why not? Either in their natural state or processed, grains and fruits were always perishable; it was safer to transport them as distilled spirits. At twenty-five cents a gallon in 1801, the market for liquor was lucrative (at the time, no commercial wine was

Keuka Lake, noted for its distinctive Y-shape.
Photo courtesy Chris Houston.

successfully produced in New York). The grain used for distilling spirits included but was not limited to barley, rye, wheat, oats, and even corn.

To make whiskey (and beer) the grain must first be malted, leading to another commercial operation that flourished during the period.

Stills notwithstanding, at a minimum of one brewery per settlement Central New York settlers brewed a great volume of beer. Barley, being relatively cold-hardy, proved a perfect crop for the region. Most early settlements had their own malt houses, which were costly to build, to accommodate cooking the barley safely. The barley crops largely went toward malting, by the hundreds of thousands of bushels each year. During harvest season, the line of farmers delivering barley every day to a malt house could be as long as a mile.

Malting and Distillation

Malting dates as far back as ancient Sumeria and Egypt, where brewing was a highly regarded trade and barley was the primary grain.

To malt, grain is harvested and dried to reduce its liquid content. It sits for a few weeks to promote seed viability. The grain is then steeped in water until the seeds sprout and the grain's moisture level is just under 50 percent by volume. The partially sprouted grain is then air-dried, followed by kiln drying to a desired toast. Malting converts starches into sugars that join the grain's small volume of natural sugars to become the food that yeasts turn into alcohol during fermentation, after water is added to make a brew. Malting also imparts intense flavors that permeate the finished product.

To make whiskey, the resulting alcoholic brew is subjected to the ancient process of distillation—essentially the process of boiling and capturing steam. Alcohol has a lower boiling point than water. Therefore, alcohol concentrates faster as vapor, which when cooled is converted into a condensed liquid with a higher alcohol ratio than the liquid that was boiled. A subsequent distillation of the condensed liquid produces steam with a higher ratio of alcohol to liquid.

The other crop necessary for beer brewing was hops.

The first record of hops used for brewing dates to around the year 1100, but the plant was in heavy use in the Middle Ages. Before the discovery of hops in brewing, a great deal of beer spoiled while and soon after it was brewed. Hops have an antibacterial capacity that attacked the microorganisms responsible for the spoilage, without attacking the yeast necessary to convert the natural sugars of the brew into alcohol. Using hops made beer better in other ways: Hops provide a bitterness that offsets the sweetness of toasted grains—the malt that is brewed to make beer—and hops react with different malts to provide the wide range of aroma and flavor characteristics in beers.

The Dutch brought hops to New Netherlands (New York) in the seventeenth century. With the influx of Europeans in the nineteenth century, hops gained and held a prominent place in the United States, more specifically in Central New York. Madison County, along the eastern border of Central New York, became the epicenter of hops production, with Onondaga County to its west in second place and Otsego and Chenango counties nearby owning their fair share of what became the largest hops production in the country.

The area's climate was as perfect for hops as the climate in northern Europe. Still, it was no easy crop. The investment and labor were formidable. The plant was grown on hills set apart from one another so that an acre of land hosted an average of eight hundred hills, which could produce as much as two thousand pounds of hops. To set new plants in recently developed hills, hops runners had to be cut underground for stems; a hops farmer waited two to four years for the first viable crop from the new plantings. While waiting for the hops to develop, many planted on the hills corn, beans, or potatoes—or all three—to have something to eat and to sell.

Hops grown in the Finger Lakes.
Courtesy Finger Lakes Farmhouse Hops.

When the hops plants began to produce, they required cultivation between the plants, along with fertilizing, insect and disease control, and training.

Hops are sometimes referred to as vines because they climb, but they are not vines; they are bines. The difference between the two is that vines produce tendrils that cling and curl as they climb; bines produce stout stems with hairs to help them climb. Hops had to be trained for climbing as soon as the fast-growing plant reached about a foot. First, a series of poles as tall as twenty feet were installed. One pole for each hill was enough to train fifteen bines. Twine was tied to the pole; the other end of the twine was tied to the hops to hold the plant upright.

Only the non-viable hop seeds of female flowers were needed for beer brewing. In autumn, the seeds were gathered by hand, brought to the dry-house, and spread on open mesh cloth in a layer up to three feet. They proceeded to dry for at least twelve hours, at temperatures no lower than 125 degrees Fahrenheit. From the dry-house, the hops were carried to a cooling location before they were sold to brewers. With a brewer in just about every community and with hops production centralized in four counties, Central and Western New York's rivers and canals were instrumental in delivering the essential ingredient for beer making. By 1879, more than thirty-nine thousand acres produced nearly twenty-two million pounds of Central New York hops for commercial breweries as well as home brewers.

From Seneca Lake to the Genesee River, farms, villages, and towns rapidly sprang up in the nineteenth century. In *Rural New York*, Fippin wrote that between 1795 and 1810, the farm population in the region had grown incredibly—from approximately twelve thousand to three hundred thousand. Yet farming remained relatively primitive. In his book, U. P. Hedrick at the Geneva Experiment Station pointed out that early-nineteenth-century farmers relied on implements that had been developed as far back as in ancient Rome. Cultivators were not in use yet; seeds of clover and grass were broadcast by hand. The sickle had just given way to the grain cradle, but harvested grain swaths were raked and bound by hand. To cut hay, the farmer used a scythe, then raked and bound the hay by hand. The corn cultivator was still some fifty years into the future; both planting and cultivating corn was accomplished with a one-horse plow. Most farmers didn't have a wheeled vehicle. Instead, they used a log sled pulled by an ox. This mode of transportation was not reserved for produce; the family used it to get to church or to other social functions.

In 1819, John Jethro Wood developed the cast-iron plow in Montville, in Cayuga County, birthplace of Millard Fillmore. To Hedrick, the invention appeared to have kicked off an inventing culture centered in that particular Finger Lakes county. To prove it, Hedrick cited the fact that by the late nineteenth century, 117 patents from Cayuga County were registered at the U.S. Patent Office. It was the largest number of farm implement inventions from one location in all of Central and Western New York.

Over at Seneca County, on a 112-acre farm with clay soil and a drainage problem, in the mid-nineteenth century a Scot named Johnson dug and put down the first tile drainage system in the Finger Lakes region, a feat that won him a silver cup from the New York Agricultural

Society. Johnson came up with the drainage idea after suffering fifteen years of poor crops because his plot of land was composed of calcareous soils of heavy clay that held water when it rained and then solidified like concrete.

In the early part of the nineteenth century, farming produced few cash crops in Central New York. When an early subsistence farmer stumbled on an occasional and diminishing population of beaver, or of fox, mink, wolf, or bear, with any luck he would have pelts to sell. Settlers also turned into cash the fish in the rivers and lakes around them—but nothing was as good a cash crop as the woodlot clearings. Settlers generally knew nothing concerning the value of potash as a soil regenerator of potassium and calcium. To them, potash was an important export cash crop. According to the author Fippin, the value of potash taken in the Genesee territory between 1805 and 1825 was put at three hundred thousand dollars.

Still, not all wood went toward potash. The wood of Central New York played a major role in cabinetry and furniture making (maple and oak), gunstocks (walnut and cherry), and coffins (pine). Wood was also needed for building material and to burn for heat. Wood fired up the steamships (and later, it fired railroad engines). Wood fired the important Salina salt mines of Syracuse, too, where about sixty cords of wood per acre, or two hundred thousand cords per year, went into the furnaces that boiled the Salina water to extract its salt. Salina salt had come a long way from its humble beginnings when post-Revolutionary settlers from all over arrived in Syracuse to boil down their own kettles of salt. By the middle of the nineteenth century, two to three million bushels annually of Salina salt traveled into Canada and all points east, and as far west to California— inside wooden barrels.

Salt sheds in Syracuse NY, from a postcard circa 1908.

Cooperage enjoyed an excellent export market, and it was the first New York industry to hire the sons of settlers as laborers. Cooperage of many shapes and sizes was needed to ship and to store the region's salt, whiskey, cider, meats, flour, vinegar, and what became a truly important commodity: maple syrup.

Tapping maple trees at the Cumming Nature Center in Naples, NY.
Courtesy VisitFingerLakes.com.

Colonists before the Revolution dreamed of developing a sugar export economy, and although they had learned from the Iroquois how to extract maple syrup, their focus was misguidedly on beets and sorghum. After the Revolution, the new settlers realized quickly that neither beets nor sorghum could ever compete with Caribbean cane sugar and molasses. Central New York settlers, however, discovered that the unique and abundant maple syrup of the region could be a wonderful export crop. Throughout the nineteenth century—and beyond—New York maple syrup was among the most important crops in the state, most of which came from Central New York.

In general, shipping anything anywhere was arduous and adventurous, but continued commercial growth in the nineteenth century would soon result in lowering the cost of shipping and improving its speed and safety.

The post-Revolution population was overwhelmingly British, Scots, and Irish. Many came direct from their homeland, but even more came from eastern US cities. German and Italian immigrants followed: By the middle of the nineteenth century, the Finger Lakes region comprised fourteen still-growing counties: Monroe, Livingston, Wayne, Ontario, Seneca, Schuyler, Yates, Chemung, and Steuben; and, to the region's east, the counties of Onondaga, Cayuga, Tompkins, Cortland, and Tioga. In many communities, farming was about to grow into an industry all its own, and the diversity in population demanded diversity in agriculture.

The Best Crops

Although the region's climate could be fickle and erratic, south of Lake Ontario and into the Genesee Valley was fertile land. Measured by the prevalence of temperatures above fifty degrees Fahrenheit, the growing season of the region averaged 160 days. Rain throughout the five months of the growing season averaged sixteen inches. Closer to Lake Ontario, the season was long enough but not too hot, with cool nights in summer as well as snow cover for protection in winter. These were perfect conditions for growing fruit trees, especially in and around Geneva.

Farm in Geneva, NY.
The Geneva area proved especially well-suited to grow crops such as barley, wheat, and oats.
Courtesy VisitFingerLakes.com

Genesee, Livingston, and Ontario counties to the southeast and southwest of Geneva proved perfectly situated for wheat and oats as well as for secondary crops like barley for malting and rye for whiskey as well as for straw as a good cover crop to improve the soil. Oats became valuable as a livestock feed crop and as a cereal crop for human consumption. Oats grew best in a cool, moist environment and could be planted early in the spring to provide a harvest while farmers waited for wheat and rye to mature after the summer. The warmer, humid summers of the lowlands south of Lake Ontario proved best for a variety of vegetables, but—as the Iroquois had already discovered—they were especially hospitable to corn (by midcentury, about forty varieties) as well as beans, squash, and cabbage.

By the middle of the century, beans, peas, and cabbage had become major crops of the Finger Lakes region. Beans and peas did particularly well in the calcareous Ontario and Honeoye soils; cabbage was suited to the mucky Clyde soils, where onion also proved successful. Situated close to Geneva, the town of Phelps became the cabbage capital of the United States, mainly turning the cruciferous leaves into sauerkraut—in the twentieth century, the Empire State Pickling Plant, at

The town of Phelps, near Geneva, became the cabbage capital of the United States in the early twentieth century and was home to the largest sauerkraut factory in the world. Here, workers in Phelps sort freshly-made sauerkraut.
Courtesy of PhelpsNY.com

Eagle Street in Phelps, was the largest sauerkraut factory in the world.

Peppermint was another important crop in the Clyde soils. In 1839, Hiram G. Hotchkiss founded the H.G. Hotchkiss International Prize Medal Essential Oil Company in Phelps. He moved the company two years later to be closer to better transportation, which he found in the village of Lyons in Wayne County situated midway between Lake Ontario and the north end of Seneca and Cayuga lakes. Legend has it that travelers from any direction knew they were approaching Lyons by the wafting peppermint aroma that filled the air. Hotchkiss became the largest essential oil company in the world, lasting in Lyons until 1982.

The Hotchkiss Essential Oil Company building as it appears today. *Courtesy LyonsNY.com*

Clover and alfalfa for hay prefers loamy soils with good lime content, the kind found throughout the Genesee Valley and in parts of Cayuga and Onondaga counties. Alfalfa growing began in 1812 and increased over the next hundred years to thirty-three thousand acres planted; the crop did well on the drumlin slopes. The Dunkirk and Ontario soils of Onondaga County proved especially good for teasel, the flower heads of which were dried and then attached to spinning devices that had been raising the nap on fabrics since classical Greece and Roman times. Teasel made its way into Central New York in 1840 from England. Outside of some teasel plantings in Oregon, until after the turn of the century, the town of Skaneateles south of Syracuse was the US center for production of this biannual crop.

After Irish immigrants brought the potato from Europe to the Northern Hemisphere of the New World in the seventeenth century, the Iroquois showed little interest in the tuber. By 1840, however, with thirty million bushels produced, the potato was among the top five New York crops. While Long Island was the largest potato-growing section of the state, the west-central plateau of northern New York proved hospitable to the tuber, though the high cost to transport the heavy and bulky crop ensured that it was grown mainly to serve the local market. The city of Naples, at Canandaigua Lake, produced and shipped more potatoes by volume than any other local community.

An Old Recipe for Homemade Sauerkraut

Ingredients

1 head green cabbage (up to 3 pounds)

1 ½ tablespoons salt

1 tablespoon caraway seeds (optional)

Equipment

Good sharp knife

Cutting board

2 wide-mouthed mason jars, 1 quart each

Mason jar funnel

2 small jars filled to the top with sterilized
   pebbles that will fit into the mason jars

Cheesecloth

Rubber bands

Directions

1. Everything must be squeaky-clean, including your hands, with no soap residue anywhere.

2. Get rid of limp cabbage outer leaves and be sure to put aside two firm outer leaves.

3. To create the "slaw" slices, cut the cabbage into quarters; remove the hard core; slice each quarter in half, lengthwise; then slice each wedge crosswise into thin strands.

4. Place the cabbage into a mixing bowl, add the salt and optional caraway seeds; working with your hands, knead for 10 minutes or until the cabbage is limp.

5. Use the funnel to pack the cabbage into the larger mason jars by hand, tamping it down every so often. When you're done, place a reserved cabbage leaf into each jar, spreading it over the sliced cabbage. Pour half the remaining liquid in the mixing bowl into one mason jar and the other half into the second; then place each of the small jars filled with pebbles over the cabbage in each mason jar, to weight it down.

6. Cover the jars with cheesecloth and secure each with a rubber band.

7. Place the jars out of direct sunlight, between 65 and 75°F. On the first day, check frequently. You want the liquid to rise over the cabbage completely, and you do this by pressing down on the jar with pebbles. If after 24 hours, the cabbage is not fully submerged, dissolve 1 teaspoon of salt in 1 cup of water; add enough of this liquid to each jar to submerge the cabbage.

8. Check the jars daily, pressing down to keep the cabbage submerged. The cabbage is fermenting, so it may produce bubbles or foam. Don't worry about it. Worry only if you see mold, which you should remove immediately.

9. After 3 days, taste the cabbage each day until it tastes the way you want it; then remove the jar with pebbles, screw on a cap, and refrigerate. Refrigerated, sauerkraut should keep for as long as 60 days.

Bopple Hill Road,
Naples, NY.
Courtesy
VisitFingerLakes.com.

Demand for Central New York produce grew as rapidly as the country's population. The largest density of people was within a five-hundred-mile-radius circle with Syracuse at its center. The circle included every state that borders New York plus good portions of New Hampshire, Rhode Island, Maine, Delaware, Maryland, Virginia, West Virginia, and Ohio. Central and Western New York farms had access to the most populous region of the country, but feeding this vast population was not the only opportunity the region had. By the late nineteenth century, the Northeast, Midwest, and parts of the Southeast had become the center for US manufacturing. A great deal of that manufacturing used farm products as its base, such as skins, pulp, stalks, and even oils. The manufacturing boom serviced that five-hundred-mile radius of an expanding population, and getting goods to the East Coast also provided access to markets across the Atlantic. Transporting farm and manufacturing products to the vast surrounding market efficiently and safely was of paramount importance, and it may not have been successful were it not for an east–west transportation route that went into operation in 1826.

Transportation

Commercial navigation of the eleven Finger Lakes began shortly after the post-Revolution settlements. The first of these was the boat *Alexander* on Seneca Lake in 1796. With their cargo of local produce and supplies, boats on the inland lakes soon became the connection among communities along the lakes' shores, but commercial expansion from lake to lake to the west or east was hindered by the often north–south configuration of most rivers, the near impassability of streams, and the narrowness of old Iroquois foot trails. Even after the trails were widened into roads built out of logs laid across the earth, traffic for horse-drawn stages was difficult: The roads were not exactly smooth, and they were blocked by snow in winter, muddy in spring, and malaria-infested in summer. Horses regularly died trying to make the journeys along roads like the Seneca Turnpike that ran from Utica west about 117 miles to Canandaigua as one in a series of turnpikes that covered about 3,000 miles of the state, complete with toll bridges.

In 1797, as part of the Seneca Turnpike system, a bridge of more than a mile went under construction across northern Cayuga Lake, where the village of Cayuga is today. The bridge was completed in 1800, collapsed in 1804, was rebuilt in 1812, and remained standing until 1857.

Despite the bridge, throughout the first decade of the nineteenth century, travel losses were extensive and of course, expensive. To send goods from Central New York east to the Hudson River region meant traveling a long, hard journey that began on the Mohawk River—and that was fraught with twists and turns, a number of necessary locks

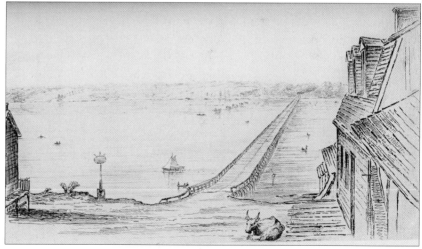

An early nineteenth-century image of the ill-fated Cayuga Lake Bridge.

that slowed traffic down, plus a series of connections to smaller waterways that had to be made, sometimes along toll roads, before the cargo reached Schenectady.

Serious talk of a canal to connect the vast expanse between the Hudson and Genesee rivers had been heard in the latter part of the eighteenth century. Politicians and businessmen even organized a few canal-building companies with all kinds of routes in mind, but by 1800 no canal was being dug. That year, Governor Morris suggested a commercial canal that would tap water from Lake Erie on the western edge of New York State and would flow east all the way to the Hudson River. His suggestion included a series of locks to accommodate the terrain. Some thought such a lengthy canal a bad idea, but those who counted—the entrepreneurial political class—got behind it. In 1808, the state assembly granted six hundred dollars (close to seventeen thousand in 2013 dollars) for preliminary surveys. In 1810, state senator and future governor DeWitt Clinton was put in charge of a survey to cut through the center of the state. By 1817, Morris's canal was being dug. The state legislature set up a special fund for the work. They placed duties on the delivery of salt, which was the first major commercial product on the new sections of canal to be built between the Mohawk and Seneca regions as well as between Lake Champlain and the Hudson River. To fund the rest of the canal project to the west, taxes were levied, lotteries devised, and tolls planned along the route. Immigrants by the hundreds kept costs down by laboring at low wages to build the canal. More money was saved by the use of prisoner labor. In the end, $8 million had been spent to build the canal by the time it was put into service in 1826 as the Erie Canal ($225 million in 2013 dollars).

LEFT
The north end of Cayuga Lake, near the area where the Cayuga Lake Bridge once stood. *Courtesy Chris Houston.*

The Erie Canal's first year was an astounding success: It almost immediately changed Western and Central New York into the commercial farming and manufacturing hub of the Northeast. All along the canal route, successful tanneries and mills were established. The lumber industry expanded greatly, too (between 1832 and 1860, Albany became the largest lumber market in North America). Wheat shipped from Rochester was another early beneficiary of the canal. The time to send flour to New York City was reduced by two-thirds, and the cost to move a ton dropped by 95 percent. Rochester produced more flour than any other city in the world, gaining the tag "Flour City." Between 1826 and 1836, the success of Rochester's wheat shipments along the canal spurred a population growth in the city of more than 400 percent. The Erie Canal also allowed Syracuse-area salt to be shipped across the country more quickly and efficiently. The population of Syracuse grew rapidly, too: nearly 300 percent between 1826 and 1836.

In 1833, a waterway outlet was officially dug from an existing stream to connect Keuka with Seneca Lake so that goods could then flow north to Geneva and to the Erie Canal. This outlet from Penn Yan to Dresden was only eight miles long, but it descended almost three hundred feet, requiring more than two dozen locks in its short run, which supported dozens of mills and distilleries. The location of the Bogert Mill, built in 1831, gave its owners control over the flow of water from the lake's outlet through the canal. With that in mind, the three Birkett brothers added to their milling enterprises in the Northeast and Midwest when they bought the Bogert Mill. Birkett Mills remains standing in Penn Yan today and is known for quality buckwheat and wheat flours; in fact, it is today the world's largest producer of buckwheat goods.

LEFT
The Erie Canal.
Courtesy
Chris Houston.

Buckwheat

Buckwheat cultivation is as old as civilization. It was first cultivated in the Balkans region and quickly became a staple, especially in the diets of Central and Eastern Asians and later Middle Easterners and then Europeans, who brought it to America from Holland.

Buckwheat is a relative of rhubarb, a native plant that grew extensively throughout Central New York. In the eighteenth century, buckwheat was a godsend for the region's settlers. It grows well in northern climates—particularly in acidic underfertilized soil, the kind found along many of the slopes and plateaus of the Finger Lakes region. It quickly became a regional staple; its stalks can be used as straw for poultry and other livestock, and it can be tilled in to help revitalize the soil. When it grows, buckwheat's density crowds out weeds, and its nitrogen-fixing qualities as well as its ability to prevent erosion make it a perfect cover crop for crop rotation.

Sown in mid-June, buckwheat blooms throughout the next ten weeks of summer, which makes it a good crop for honeybees. The flowers yield the buckwheat kernels known as groats, which can be cooked whole, as cereal, or milled into flour to make pancakes and other baked goods.

The Finger Lakes region became a maze of smaller dug waterways to connect southern areas with northern ports on the Erie Canal; among the first was a waterway that connected Cayuga Lake. Another important waterway connected Elmira and the Chemung River to Watkins Glen. Before the last two were connected, millions of board feet of lumber were floated on the Chemung to the Susquehanna to points south. After the waterway was opened to the north, a great deal of that lumber was diverted to eastern markets via the Erie Canal. The small waterway between Keuka and Seneca lakes may have been successful at trafficking goods from Keuka Lake to the Erie Canal port at Geneva, but it did little to help get product onto the boats for farmers located many miles south of Keuka. More shipments of goods to New York City displaced shipments from Bath down the Cohocton to the Susquehanna River. The Erie Canal was, in part, the cause of a local economic depression in the Bath area. The once dynamic pace at the southern portion of the old Pulteney Estate was slowed. This was not the case for the rest of the region. Before the Erie Canal, crops in Western and Central New York were grown on a small scale to feed the family or else on a medium-large scale to feed the local community. The canal increased demand, and that made New York State number one in farm products—a position the state held until after the Civil War.

Despite its immediate success, the Erie Canal faced a competitive threat almost right away. No sooner was the canal put into service than, in 1826, the Mohawk Hudson Rail Company was chartered; its first train run, from Albany to Schenectady powered by steam, took place in August 1831. The rail line was intended as a supplement to the canal system and as such, tracks were not allowed to parallel the waterway.

The first railroad of Western New York went into service at Rochester in 1832 to connect with Buffalo; it, too, was powered by steam. Between 1832 and 1851, a series of rail connections joined important commercial centers between Western and Central New York and all the way to Albany. It took a full day to make the trip. In 1851, the travel time was cut to twelve hours after the Erie Railroad, traveling along the southern tier near the border with Pennsylvania, became the first line to cross the entire state from New York City, with its last stop at Dunkirk near Lake Erie. The New York Central line followed in 1853; it was then consolidated into five lines that took passengers from New York City into the Midwest. Traveling along the Hudson and then west to the Great Lakes regions, the New York Central paralleled the canal route. The rail system in New York was complete by 1880. Fifteen years later, it was electrified and moved both people and cargo regularly. For a time, the canal maintained its importance, but by 1902 the railroad had won out.

Although the Erie Canal and its tributary waterways connected Central and Western New York to the rest of world, the railroad was important during the region's shift from agrarian supremacy to industrial power because it was faster and more efficient. (As a benefit of the railroad, time used to be kept locally, but the railroad's need for accurate and consistent timekeeping gave us the Eastern Standard Time system.) The railroad's best advantage over the canal system was that it could provide unbroken service in winter, unlike the canal, which froze and thawed, and froze and thawed throughout the cold months. While it became the engine for industrial expansion, the railroad continued to offer benefits to farmers as well. Before it was electrified, its need for wood created a market for timber at rail stops all along each route. Farmers received ready cash as the stationmaster contracted and paid for stacks of forest timber, which though diminished was still in relative abundance across Central New York. By opening up forestland for tracks, the railroad also cleared more land for agriculture.

The only downside of the railroad for farmers was that the explosion in demand made some regret giving up right-of-way through land that they might have been able to make productive.

From Farm to Industrial Revolution

The materials of manufacturing are the products of the farm, the forest, the stream, the mine and the quarry . . . the transfer of others as a result of changed natural advantages.

—*Rural New York* by Elmer Otterbein Fippin

To illustrate what he meant, Fippin pointed to tobacco farming and manufacturing.

In New York State, the tobacco industry was centered in the Finger Lakes County of Chemung. Tobacco farming began there in 1850, in the county's vast alluvial soil area known as Big Flats. This area hosts one of the oldest Native American village sites in New York, Runonvea, where prehistoric Lamoka stone tools, axes, and arrowheads have been uncovered, and where Sullivan's army found and burned an Iroquois village in 1779.

Post-Revolutionary Big Flats settlers relied economically on lumber. Later, thanks to the alluvial soils, hay and dairy products supplied the largest cheese company in the southern tier, Pollyo, and its famous Italian-style cheeses (the factory is now owned by Kraft Foods).

By the start of the American Civil War, Big Flats farmers were harvesting, drying, and selecting more than a quarter million pounds of tobacco. The Brand family of Elmira did much to advance tobacco farming and to sell tobacco on the market. In 1870, John Brand established packing and processing houses in the area to sort and grade Big Flats tobacco for sale to cigar manufacturers.

Designed for producing cigars, the Chemung County tobacco industry began to fail in the early twentieth century as cigarettes, produced mainly in the South, gained commercial dominance. The Finger Lakes tobacco industry was on its slide downward by 1920; the last tobacco harvest came in 1950, a century after the first one. Yet no other activity in the region better reflects how an agricultural product made its way from the farm to industry.

At the start of the twentieth century, with two thousand acres of cultivated tobacco, Big Flats supported as many as two hundred tobacco farmers and between one and two thousand full- and part-time field pickers and cigar-manufacturing plant workers. Chemung County was home to ten cigar-rolling plants in Elmira plus four plants in Big Flats, each located as close to the Erie Railroad as they could get—some right along the tracks.

RIGHT
Lively Run Dairy's
Cayuga Blue in
its first stages of
aging.
*Courtesy Lively Run
Goat Dairy.*

The railroad is credited with much of the state's industrial success as the nineteenth gave way to the twentieth century. Industries flourishing in Western and Central New York included 10 percent of the nation's manufacture of boots and shoes and the majority of the nation's glove making in an area that was known as the leather-stocking district. The central-western portion of the state accounted for 60 percent of the value of woven goods; a major dried-fruit industry from apples as well as berries; a multitude of mills handling not only the state's crops of buckwheat, wheat, corn, and other grains and seeds, but also milled livestock feed crops from outside the state for a growing New York dairy industry; large limestone and shale stock mining for cement; gypsum mining from the Salina formation that was used for fertilizer; natural gas mined in Onondaga County; and 17 percent of the nation's cooperage, which of course held all that flour the city of Rochester produced as well as the region's maple sugar, fresh fruit, cider, wine from the Finger Lakes wine industry that had developed in the 1860s—and of course tobacco.

In Western and Central New York, the railroad certainly played a major role in the success of three particular farm-based industries that ultimately gained national (and international) prominence: dairy, apples, and grapes.

3

Land of Milk and Cheese

All civilized people use milk from farm animals. The more highly civilized and prosperous the population, the greater is the amount of milk consumed.
—*Dairy Farming* by C.H. Eckles and G.F. Warren

Throughout Central New York today, luxuriant pastures share space with neatly patterned farmland. Some of the pasture was there when the settlers arrived; some was created as settlers felled more and more of the deciduous and evergreen forests. Pasture often flourishes on the least crop-friendly locations, and the Lake Ontario region is home to bluegrass pasture that makes a wonderful natural livestock feed.

The marriage of pasture with the long hours of feed-crop farming gave rise to husbandry as a means of providing protein and dietary fats without having to wander into the forests to hunt. Pigs, mostly in the form of salt pork, were an important protein source to settlers from the start, but hogs gave no milk. Fowl mainly provided the concentrated fat and protein of eggs, and its meat was not beyond a settler's reach (some of the oldest White Leghorn poultry breeds were established around Cayuga Lake, where the Black Cayuga duck also originated). Sheep were important, too, for wool for a spring lamb to grace the table now and again and to a lesser degree for milk. Sheep produce a small volume of low-fat milk for cheese making, and while the sheep industry has not been historically as large and economically viable as the bovine milk industry, in the early twentieth century Central New York was home to about 20 percent of the state's sheep herds as opposed to less than 10 percent of the state's bovine herds.

It finally became clear, however, that no animal was as valuable as the bovine for providing high-quality protein food sources in large volume.

Why Milk?

In the early nineteenth century, few raised beef cattle, but just about every Central New York farm had a dairy cow or two to help feed the family. Raising beef simply did not pay off. The amount of feed needed to grow a steer to twelve hundred pounds produced only one-third as much food for humans as it did when fed to a dairy cow. Even if Central New York farmers wanted to raise beef, for high quality the animals require a warmer climate and different types of feed than that available in Great Lakes areas. Finally, to get beef from a steer, the farmer had to slaughter the animal into which he had invested time and money; cattle thus had to be transported live over long distances and then slaughtered—the cost was high. After the introduction of refrigerated rail cars, it was safer and smarter to transport milk to markets than it was to transport animals, and the best thing going for the dairy cow was that it produced milk year after year.

Central New York farm families came to need the dairy cow. Sheep could not provide as much milk as the cow, and although it was second to the dairy cow for protein, the pig (as well as fowl hens) required a better class of food to survive than the dairy cow. The dairy cow was most efficient at converting grass, hay, straw, and cornstalks, as well as brewing and mill by-products. into high-quality milk for human consumption.

In human food energy, the dairy cow returned almost 50 percent of what it digested; the pig, which was second to the cow, returned about 30 percent. Like no other liquid, cow's milk provided as much as 13 percent highly digestible dry matter; a quart of milk provided almost half as much protein as a pound of sirloin; and a pound of butter provided almost four times as much energy. Finally, according to author Fippin, scientists discovered that 100 pounds of plant feed got a farmer 5.1 pounds of egg nutrition from fowl, 15.6 pounds of nutrition from pigs, 2.6 pounds from sheep, and 2.8 pounds from beef cattle—but from dairy cows a whopping 18 pounds of milk, from which could be drawn 5.4 pounds of butter and 9.4 pounds of cheese.

As a bonus, dairy cattle produced manure in large volume, and because it contained vegetative waste, it restored farm soil fertility like no other animal's waste product.

All the advantages of dairy farming over beef were accented by one major advantage: In the mid-nineteenth century, the demand for dairy products spiked in proportion to the rate of growth of cities in the United States; like produce farmers, Central and Western New York dairy farmers were situated in the middle of that most densely populated five-hundred-mile radius of demand. The most important city to a New York farmer was New York City, which could be serviced easily by farmers in the Hudson Valley, just a few hours north of the city; this is where the state's commercial milk industry first gained success. Yet Central New York farmers were not left out. They were able to expand both their market for milk and their reach after the development of corn silage technology that allowed efficient winter milk production along with the introduction of refrigerated rail transportation so that their milk could reach a good portion of that five-hundred-mile radius.

No matter the promise of late-nineteenth-century dairy farming, it still took a risk-taking entrepreneur mentality to go forward—qualities that the region had produced before and was about to produce again. Dairy farming required feed crops, extensive acreage, and buildings with construction specialized to accommodate housing, cleaning, and milking cows. Before a produce crop farmer added dairy farming to his vocation, the farmer's financial situation had to be analyzed. A dairy farm needed to strike the right balance with the proper size of the business, the best return on production per cow, good feed crop management, and the incorporation of cash crop farming into the milk production schedule. The nature of milk production and pricing was such that the smaller the farm, the less likely it was to succeed. An early-twentieth-century study covering Tompkins, Livingston, and Jefferson counties presented in Eckles and Warren's *Dairy Farming* showed that a two-hundred-acre dairy farm grossed almost ten times more income than a thirty-acre farm, with only twice the amount of human effort. The study also showed that the machinery costs on the small farm were double the cost per acre than on the larger farm. An average 150 to 200 acres seemed to be the best size for a diversified cash crop/dairy farm. Crops on such a farm in Central New York might include corn for silage, timothy and alfalfa for hay, wheat, oats, potatoes, and two important regional cash crops, cabbage and apples.

Red cabbage in the Finger Lakes. Cabbage was an important cash crop for Finger Lakes farmers in the late nineteenth century and continues to be grown in the region today. *Courtesy VisitFingerLakes.com.*

The farmer who didn't have enough land would have to decide either to buy or to lease land. Once land was secured, the next task was to design and build a large milking and herding barn. In most cases, the barn had to be at least eighty feet long and nearly sixty feet wide, to accommodate half the herd on each wall and enough room for wagon traffic in the middle (for cleaning and manure gathering), but not so much room that lighting the barn became expensive and problematic. As much natural sunlight as possible was good, but not always practical. For cleanliness, a floor of concrete was preferred but wood was better than no floor at all, and gutters were required. Stalls needed to be three to four feet wide, depending on the breed of cow, and the feeding manger had to be concrete. At the turn of the century, erecting a proper barn (plus milking room and silo) could cost anywhere between fifty and a hundred dollars per cow, depending on whether it was to be a barn strictly to sell milk to market or a barn for a dairy farm that sold milk to a creamery for processing, and whether the herd was of valuable purebred stock.

The New York State Agricultural Experiment Station

In 1880, the New York legislature proposed what became the fourth agricultural institution in America. After much wrangling, the law was passed the following year, and the New York State Agricultural Experiment Station was established on a farm in Geneva. The year after that, the state took title to the land. Everyone from farmers to newspaper editors had an idea what the station should do and how it should go about its business, but in the end the station became part of Cornell University's horticultural department with a mandate to investigate soil technology, plant breeding, and entomology as these related to farm crops.

From the beginning, the experiment station became the focus of agricultural information and learning. Farmers had access to the station's no-nonsense, readable bulletins, issued to report on the results of its work in the laboratory and in the field. The station's influence helped farming communities along the Erie Canal's path develop crops most suitable to their environment. Later, the agricultural station involved itself with livestock.

Cattle were not native to the United States. That fact, and the fact that originally, milk commanded a flat price by the pound, made it an imperative to look for and find the breed that would give farmers high production at the lowest possible cost. Dairy breeds that became common in the US included Holstein and Belted (Dutch), Ayrshire (Scottish), Jersey and Guernsey (British), and Brown Swiss. At an average of twelve hundred pounds per cow and two thousand pounds per bull, the Dutch Holstein was the first dairy breed to prove successful in New York. Holsteins also produced more milk per cow than other breeds. The major Holstein downside was that the milk was the lowest in fat, which meant it was not the best for producing the higher-income-producing butter and cheese.

The research of the first director at the Geneva Agricultural Experiment Station, Dr. E. Lewis Sturdevant, showed that the English Channel breeds Jersey and Guernsey produced a high volume of quality butterfat for the lowest cost of production. Milk casein is white, but most milk fat comes with a yellow hue—carotin—a reflection of the plant life on which cows are fed. Guernseys produced the best yellow milk fat, too, which lent nothing to quality but everything to marketing as its cream and butterfat products were attractive to consumers.

Sturdevant's discovery would likely not have been possible had it not been for the research of his colleague at the station, chemist and New York native son Stephen Moulton Babcock. The combined work of the two men led to improvements in dairy herds, dairy manufacturing reforms and controls, and milk purity regulations. More important, out of the work of the two men came a change in the way milk was priced. Rather than being paid by the pound for their milk, farmers received payment based on the quality and volume of butterfat content. This change alone reduced the number of Holstein herds and increased the number of Guernsey herds in Central New York, and it created a powerful dairy industry.

Because the market for milk was so large in the growing northeastern cities, the economy of scale was much better suited to the volume of milk produced by cows than by any other animal, but only providing those dairy farmers had milk to sell all year round.

Corn field, Ontario County, NY.
Courtesy VisitFingerLakes.com.

In the southern states, dairy farms often included more cattle than the acreage of forage crops indicated, because in the South cows could feed from pastures for most of the year. It was generally understood that cool regions were more suitable to raising dairy cattle, since moisture made pasture and other feed crops more abundant, and although the lime content of Central New York soil made its bluegrass a prime pasture feed, the region was sometimes problematically cold. Farmers had to give thought to the quality and availability of feed crops so that milk could be produced in winter as well as in summer. For this information, the Geneva Agricultural Experiment Station was again a valuable resource. Work at the station focused on cattle nutrition, and climate suitability for feed crops.

Dairy farms made good use of the return that hay provided in manure from cows to produce quality cash crops like potatoes, cabbages, and sweet corn for human consumption. Central New York's climate and topography delivered beautiful alfalfa, clover, and timothy hay crops (south of Lake Ontario where it grew abundantly, alfalfa was preferred). But the problem in New York was the price of hay, which by the early twentieth century had outpaced the price of hay in the West by as much as 86 percent. Storing bales of hay in the barn loft was an easy and cost-effective way to handle the winter feed crop, and so scientists at Geneva made it clear to farmers that good pasture was always part of the mix, but storage capacity was necessary to produce winter milk to increase the annual dairy profit. By the late nineteenth century, it was a given that to generate enough income from northeastern dairy farming, access to a silo was crucial.

Hay bales, Ontario County, NY.
Courtesy VisitFingerLakes.com.

Silo construction was not exactly cheap. How profitable silage feeding was had to do with the size of the herd. It was not cost-effective to build a silo to feed fewer than twenty cattle. The authors of *Dairy Farming* recount that in the early twentieth century, only 7 percent of dairy farms in Livingston County with fewer than fifteen milking cows relied on silage as feed, whereas 83 percent of dairy farms in the county with more than twenty-five milking cows used silage. Dairy farms were large enterprises by design. Still, the silage system initiated rapid growth in the Central New York dairy industry, and since the silo for winter feed was filled mostly with corn, corn growers benefited, too. Corn was the best crop for silage. Even in years where the summers proved too short to mature corn, the stalks could be used in the silo. Before this growth in the dairy industry, the acreage of corn grown in Central New York had been declining, since farmers had been hurt by railroad deliveries of large volumes of corn grown in the more temperate western and southwestern portions of the country. The introduction of the silo started to turn that situation around. (Although hay remained expensive, some quality hay was necessary, as was wheat bran and even grain by-products from nearby breweries to balance proteins and reduce carbohydrates when corn was used as feed.)

As a bonus, dairying benefited the pork industry, too. Until New York pork was overtaken in the twentieth century by meat from the

West in greater abundance than the East seemed able to provide, the New York pig fattened well on milk fat products provided by the dairy cow. Estimates are that on a late-nineteenth-century Central New York dairy farm, one pig was counted among every four dairy cows.

Butter and Cheese

Whole-milk products largely reflect the relationship between fat and sugar. Milk sugar changes into lactic acid—sour milk—when lactose is exposed to certain bacteria. When butter is churned from milk, the sugar goes into the skimmed portion of the milk and into the "buttermilk." Butter is composed of very little milk sugar. The fact that Guernseys became the dominant breed in Central New York certainly placed a high value on fat or cream, and that was an opportunity to increase the relatively easy production of butter. From the latter part of the nineteenth into the twentieth century, more than 60 percent of the butter on the market had been produced right on the dairy farms: The cream was allowed to rise to the top of the milk for churning into butter.

Demand for milk was generally constant, but the price of milk production went up in winter. Although the price that farmers received was higher in December than it was in June, it was not so much higher as to make up for the increased feed and labor costs that winter milk production created. On the other hand, most of the butter that went to market was produced between May and November. It behooved dairy farmers to produce as much butter as they could during pasture months, because it could be stored, and storage helped keep the price generally stable through the seasons. Some time after 1885, the centrifugal cream separator was introduced; it allowed for faster, more efficient, and better-quality butter making. As an added bonus, mechanical separating left behind higher-quality fat-free buttermilk and skim milk products. By the early part of the twentieth century, external creameries took over the process from local farms. Creameries could best control the bacteria ripening process in butter making, and farmers received a good price for milk.

That same cream could be turned into cheese and creameries could theoretically handle the cheese, but that product had its own special manufacturing process.

An Old Recipe for Homemade Cheese

Ingredients

2 quarts fresh, whole milk

½ cup buttermilk

1 ½ teaspoons lemon juice

1 teaspoon salt

Equipment

Pot with a thick bottom to hold 2 quarts

Thermometer

Cheesecloth

Large spoon

String

Directions

1. Pour the milk into the pot and heat to 175°F—***do not boil it***. When the temperature is right, pour in the buttermilk and lemon juice; turn off the heat and watch the milk separate into solid curds and liquid whey. Let rest for 10 minutes.

2. While you're waiting, line two layers of cheesecloth in a colander, over a bowl. After 10 minutes are up, put in the curds with a large spoon; let all the excess liquid drain into the bowl, then let the curds rest for about 5 more minutes.

3. Lift the cheesecloth to form a bundle, tie it with string, and hang the bundle over the bowl for a final liquid drain for up to 45 minutes.

4. Mix the salt into the cheese (don't worry about the curd breaking).

5. The new cheese can be smoothed out and eaten fresh, or it can be wrapped well in a ramekin and refrigerated to meld and develop a richer flavor. Prepare or serve the cheese any way that you would prepare or serve cream, cottage, or Italian ricotta cheese.

Makes about 2 pounds of cheese

Even with refrigeration, it still was best to be as close as possible to the population that demanded fresh milk. This was not the case for cheese, which could last much longer on a journey to more distant markets. By 1850, Central New York counties of Madison, Chenango, and Otsego sent almost twenty-five million pounds of cheese to Albany. By the late nineteenth century, the fertile, rich pasture south of Lake Ontario between Syracuse and Utica and into the region's southern tier at Chemung County—where good rainfall allowed for natural pasture as well as the largest acreage of alfalfa—made Central New York along with the rest of the Great Lakes region the dairy capital of the country. And the focus was more and more on cheese.

Cheese production flourished in cool regions with especially limestone-rich soils, which of course described the pastures south of Lake Ontario. At first, the cheese in Central New York was produced on individual farms for family and for local community consumption. Its quality was generally good, as far as local consumption demanded. From on-the-farm cheese making came small enterprises that gathered up excess milk to make cheese that was then sold in local urban markets, sometimes as far away as New York City and even for export. In the early days, relatively primitive production practices coupled with a disregard for cleanliness of the small operations held back progress.

The first successful cheese factory in the United States was built in 1851 in Oneida County, on a more-than-250-acre farm in Rome, east of Syracuse. From the milk of his family's cows, Jesse Williams produced a cheddar cheese modeled after the cheese that was produced in New England at the time from recipes brought to the New World on the *Mayflower*. After winning an award in 1850 for his cheddar, and facing increased demand, Williams sought ways to increase production as well as quality, which led to him inventing a machine that made cheese in uniform blocks on a large scale. He bought up larger volumes of milk from area farmers and created the first American association of cheese manufacturers with the sole purpose of developing an American (mainly New York) cheese production industry to rival Europe. Within fifteen years, five hundred cheese manufacturers graced New York State, with most centered in the Mohawk Valley. The flourishing cheese industry relied extensively on local dairy farmers as well as milk from farmers to the valley's west and in the pasture-rich southern tier of the Finger Lakes region.

Jesse Williams, creator of one of the first cheese factories in the United States. *Courtesy Oneida County Historical Society.*

Following the success of the Williams cheese factory, a Herkimer County resident who studied law at Hamilton College, Xerxes A. Willard, somehow got himself into agriculture with an emphasis on cheese. It started with his first of many essays regarding the Herkimer County dairy industry. In 1864, Willard gave the principal address at the New York

State Cheese Makers' Association meeting in Utica (later to become the American Dairymen's Association). Willard warned that as successful as New York cheese had become, imported European cheese remained a threat, especially after prices would fall following the American Civil War and as long as the quality of English cheddar remained far superior to New York's version. The association sent Willard to England in 1866 on a fact-finding trip that solidified his resolve to get New York cheese makers to upgrade their production practices. He particularly homed in on the difference between the way New York and British cheese makers handled the curd.

In New York, curd was stirred. The resulting cheese retained too much liquid (whey and water), and that was a condition for unwanted fermentation, especially after the cheese was sent to market. Many New York cheeses on their way to urban markets or for export fell apart in transit as they fermented and crumbled. Real English cheese was produced with a method simply called cheddaring, a process that, rather than stirring the curd, matted it together after the liquid was drawn off. Better expulsion of liquid resulted in a more evenly defined lactic acid development for fermentation to complete and not restart in transit. In addition, unlike the various sizes and shapes of New York stirred curd cheddar, English cheddar blocks were nearly uniform; they made a better presentation in the market. In fact, the term *American cheese* gained its derogatory connotation during the nineteenth century in England, referring to the lumpy, flaky, unreliable "cheddar" from New York. The later emergence of large-scale manufacturers, like Kraft, that produced slices of processed cheese reinforced the already established negative reputation of American cheese, but for a different reason.

Despite the problems, New York cheese production and marketing had been succeeding even before the production upgrade, so much so that two important dairy exchanges were situated near the heavily trafficked Syracuse, with its easy access to the railroad. Part of that success was thanks to the cheese commission house of Harry Burrell. Burrell was a resident of Little Falls, New York, but he established his company in New York City. Solely on commission, Burrell and Company sold cheese in the city and for export. The company moved many tons of cheese through the great city and on ships. In 1858, Harry's seventeen-year-old son David Burrell joined the company as a cheese salesman. Ten years later, David was on a trip to England where, like

Xerxes Willard who'd made the trip two years earlier, he saw firsthand the quality and uniform size of British cheddar cheese, but he did not fixate on how curd was handled.

David Burrell came home from his trip to England convinced that not just cheese, but the overall New York dairy industry needed better manufacturing equipment. With a partner, he opened a shop in his hometown of Little Falls to service the dairy industry with the best equipment available. He was an avid promoter of the silage system in 1880 so that milking could take place all year round. In 1881, Burrell introduced to New York the first centrifugal cream separator. The shop's success led the D. H. Burrell Company in 1885 to design, produce, and sell dairy equipment and supplies. Of all the bulk milk storage tanks, heat exchangers, processing vats, pumps, pipes, and conveyers that D. H. Burrell produced, the company's best-known product was the Burrell Milking Machine.

After David Burrell died in 1919, his brother Loomis ran the business with David Junior until 1928, when it was merged and became the Cherry-Burrell Corporation. Over the next five decades, the company filed and was granted numerous patents for improvements to its milking machines. Through its years of success, the Burrell family's business expanded in parallel with the growth of cheese production in and outside Central New York. The Cherry-Burrell Corporation became a national company and is today Waukesha Cherry-Burrell/ SPX of Delevan, Wisconsin, which is no surprise. In the early twentieth century, 850,000 cows produced the milk that went toward nearly 80 percent of the nation's cheese production. Many of those dairy cows were on New York farms, but a great deal of them lived in Wisconsin, the next great cheese state.

The first major threat to Central New York cheese came out of Canada, where, based on his training in Herkimer County, New York native Harry Farrington started a cheese factory in Ontario in 1864. Just over a dozen years later, 350 Canadian cheese factories vied for the New York market. By 1891, the number of Canadian cheese producers exceeded the number of cheese producers in New York by more than 50 percent.

In 1870, two New Yorkers, Chester Hazen and John J. Smith, brought New York's cheese factory technology to Wisconsin. Theirs was the first cheese shipment from Wisconsin to the New York City market. Within a few years, a Wisconsin cheese won first prize at the first International Dairy Festival, held in New York City; in 1878, the largest and most effective competition to Central New York cheese had begun to take form. The total number of cheese factories peaked in New York State around 1892. By the end of the nineteenth century, the number of cheese factories in Wisconsin surpassed that in New York. The same railroad system that helped bring Central New York cheese to prominence is implicated in the cheese industry's decline. Refrigerated railcars extended the reach of cheese, which could withstand travel to even greater distances than milk or cream.

Another dairy product that could be stored and shipped long distances was the condensed milk that Gail Borden had produced for the first time in 1853 after discovering how to heat, cleanse, and reduce water from milk without scorching it. By the Civil War period, Borden had established in the Hudson Valley the largest condensed milk factory in the world, accepting as much as twenty thousand gallons of milk each day from more than two hundred dairy farms across New York State. At the turn of the century, butter production had increased by 9 percent and cheese by 7 percent, but in the three decades immediately after the Civil War, the volume of condensed milk produced in the United States was up by 165 percent. Because it could endure longer distances than whole milk, it was common for cream to be shipped five hundred miles. The outside limit for milk shipments was about three hundred miles; for Central New York farmers that was within striking distance of the Hudson Valley, where Borden's condensed milk factory was originally located. It was simpler and faster for many Central New York dairy farmers to engage in the fresh milk market rather than in the butter or cheese market, and so the increasing demand for condensed milk lured more and more dairy farmers. Soon, at the expense of cheese production, whole milk dominated Central New York dairy shipments.

The change from controlling production locally to selling milk and cream wholesale to creameries and dealers was not without its problems for farmers. Recognizing their need to maintain a good share of the milk profits, New York's Orange County dairy farmers increased bargaining power in 1907 by creating the Dairymen's League. By 1917, after fully realizing the extent to which milk was subject to fluctuating commodity prices, dairy cooperatives became political entities. On the eve of the Great Depression, league membership was more than one hundred thousand farms, situated mostly in the east and northeastern part of the state. To guarantee a market for members, the league had developed more than 250 processing and manufacturing plants under the brand name Dairylea but had reduced that number in 1936 to just over 100. When Depression-era milk prices plummeted, independent dairy farmers in Western New York felt that dealer leagues like the Dairymen's were doing the bidding for three large companies—United States Dairy Products Company, Borden's Condensed Milk Company, and Sheffield Farms Milk Company—in a cozy relationship that suppressed milk prices further. The Western New York Milk Producers Association went on a four-day strike; it was the beginning of many years of strife for the New York dairy industry, and it caused major disruptions in New York's independent milk farming system.

In 1939, a federal court in New York shot down a milk price marketing order, once again suppressing the prices that dealers paid to milk farmers. Soon, the Supreme Court reinstated the marketing order, but the reinstatement took place when dairy production was threatened by a summer drought. In mid-August, the Dairy Farmers Union led the largest milk strike ever; it started with an August 3 vote to strike in Canton, New York, unless milk prices were changed to meet farmers' demands. By the end of August, after much violence, the strike proved successful when New York City Mayor La Guardia brokered a deal that gave the farmers the price they sought. Unfortunately, milk dealers did not live up to the agreement. Instead, they worked to break the Dairy Farmers Union, at which they succeeded in 1940 by slandering the union's leader and splitting the union into factions.

In the 1950s and '60s, dairy cooperatives found themselves in a bad spot. As markets grew larger, the number of milk-buying companies was shrinking. Cooperatives had to compete for business. Most Central New York milk was shipped in small-sized cans that farmers could fill on the farm. New regulations mandated that all milk had to be consolidated into large tanker shipments that were more easily monitored for quality and product safety. The mandate put a strain on dairy farmers who had to join with others to consolidate shipments to fill tank cars. The mandate also had the effect of lowering the price paid for milk. Between the 1960s and '70s, Central New York dairy farmers either went out of business or were forced to add a new revenue stream to their farming.

The scenario was a near death knell to New York cheese production.

According to self-published author Milton Sernett's *Say Cheese: The Story of the Era When New York State Cheese Was King,* in the 1970s,

New York held third place in cheese production, behind Wisconsin and Michigan; in the 1980s, New York slipped to fourth place; in the 1990s, New York was back in third place, but by 2008, the state had again slipped to fourth. While dairy farming is the largest agricultural industry in New York State today, accounting for more than 50 percent of agricultural revenue—the state ranks number three in US dairy production, with more than seven thousand dairy farms and nearly seven hundred thousand milking cows—instead of cheese, the state's main dairy product is fluid milk.

As a whole, New York produces less cheese in the twenty-first century than it did in the late nineteenth century; the Finger Lakes region may soon prove the exception. Dairy-farming families in the region, some with roots in dairy farming that go back to the nineteenth century, never got over the fact that after the government stepped into the market, and after the unions were beaten, dairy farming became a benevolent form of indentured living. Farmers sign an annual contract with large milk dealers, guaranteeing they will sell all their milk to that dealer, and the dealer guarantees to take the milk. The contract is silent on price, which is left to the dealer's discretion based on the dealer's perception of the cost of production for any given cycle of delivery. Farmers have no price negotiating power. If the farmer wants out of the contract, a six-month notice does the trick, and then the farmer is free to find a market for milk or cream.

A short while back, some Finger Lakes dairy farmers began to wonder how they could improve their revenue stream. What happened next appears in a future chapter.

4

Fruitful Shores

The great fruit market of the world is the American work-
man, and his staple fruit is the apple.
—*The Apple Industry of Wayne and Orleans Counties
New York,* a thesis by George Friedrich Warren, 1905

NORTH AMERICA'S INDIGENOUS APPLE is the crab apple.
Cultivated edible apples entered the New World by way of the
Mayflower. Unfortunately, the earliest apple trees brought in from
Europe didn't produce much until honeybees were also brought in
from England. Apples got to New York by way of Massachusetts,
and so did the honeybees.

The Iroquois had organized fruit orchards as early as 1743 but
relied on indigenous pollinators until the arrival of honeybees, which
the Iroquois referred to as "English flies." Thirty-six years later, during
General Sullivan's violent expedition through the southern tier of the
Finger Lakes region, troops made note of the many fruiting apple
trees they encountered—and burned.

Luckily, the apple trees were not wiped out completely.

Fruit Orchard

Post-Revolutionary Central New York settlers maintained what was
referred to as a kitchen orchard. After clearing most uncultivated
apple and pear trees to build their homes and barns, they either
kept a few trees standing or dropped seeds around their homes
expecting new ones to take root. The trees that did sprout were
allowed to take care of themselves. If a tree produced fruit, the
settlers gathered the apples and pears to feed the pigs and to make
fruit brandy and cider.

Flowering fruit trees are pollinated within their species: A pear doesn't pollinate with an apple, but separate apple varieties can and do cross-pollinate. Since the seeds from the apple of a cross-pollinated tree contain both parents, planting that seed does not come with a guarantee concerning which parent's makeup will dominate and grow into the new tree. In horticultural terms, seeds may not "grow true." The only way to know for sure which tree your new plant will become is to graft the scion wood of the tree variety that you want onto an apple tree rootstock of proven endurance in your soil. Above the graft, you get the apple that you desire; below it, you get the durable root system that you need.

Propagating fruit trees by grafting onto a scion wood stock is an ancient practice; it's mentioned in the Old and New Testaments, in Islamic texts, and in a variety of ancient gardening and agricultural periodicals and newsletters. But with North American settlers' focus on maintaining fruit trees to feed pigs and to produce cider, grafting was viewed as time consuming and unnecessary. Even the avid and gifted gardener Thomas Jefferson believed that grafted trees were not as healthy as cultivars from seed, which is how he preferred to propagate the nearly two hundred separate fruit tree cultivars at Monticello. Resistance to grafting did not break down fully in America until the mid-nineteenth century, when commercial apple farming began to take off. Since relying on seed cultivation for commercial fruit trees proved problematic, grafting catapulted the apple into a farming industry. Seventy years after its introduction, the apple was ninth in US farm crops, behind wheat, oats, cotton, corn, potatoes, barley, hay, and tobacco. Western New York became an important fruit region and among the largest for apple production in the country.

In the Finger Lakes region, overall commercial fruit production picked up after H.H. Doolittle of Oaks Corners, just northwest of Geneva, discovered around 1850 that he could propagate the wild black raspberry from the plant's tips. With extensive promotion, Doolittle's Improved Blackcap black raspberries were soon on the market toward developing a successful and sizable black raspberry industry in Wayne County and in parts of Yates County (dried raspberry tips sold for cultivation as well). The earliest known commercial sale of Central New York apples took place in 1843, with a shipment of Ontario County apples to New York City via the Erie Canal.

Homemade Hard Apple Cider

If you buy apple juice, make sure it is fresh and not pasteurized. If you juice your own, use a good juicing variety. It takes about thirty-six apples to give a gallon of juice. The other ingredients and equipment is available from home winemaker/brewer shops.

Ingredients

1 gallon apple juice
1 packet "champagne" yeast

Equipment

Sterilizing cleanser
Funnel
2 glass carboys (1 gallon each), with lids
Half-pint jar with lid

Measuring cup
Rubber bung to fit the gallon carboys
Air lock
½-inch tubing

Directions

1. First, sterilize everything, then funnel the juice into one of the glass carboys, leaving 1 cup of juice; pour this into the half-pint glass jar and freeze for later.

2. Rehydrate the yeast in the measuring cup according to instructions on the packet; then add the yeast to the juice in the bottle. Fit the bung and air lock into the carboy opening, and slowly add some water to the air lock about midway.

3. Put the carboy somewhere so that any bubbling over during fermentation can be captured and cleaned up or drained—keep it at room temperature until fermentation takes hold (1 to 2 days). When fermentation begins, put the carboy in a dark spot between 55 and 60°F. Fermentation produces carbon dioxide, which releases as bubbles through water in the air lock; check the water level daily and keep it constant.

4. Fermentation will take from 1 to 3 months. After 3 weeks, thaw the juice you froze and add it to the fermenting cider. This will reenergize the fermentation and get it as high as possible in alcohol (the top level can reach about 8.5 percent by volume). Reinstall the bung and air lock.

5. Fermentation is complete when the tiny bubbles become close to imperceptible in the air lock (a little carbon dioxide will remain in the cider, and that's good—it can protect the cider from oxidizing too quickly). Siphon the cider into a clean carboy by inserting the tube into the cider but not all the way to the bottom—you don't want the sediment. Situate the empty carboy well below the full one so that gravity transfers all the cider into the clean vessel.

Refrigerate and drink within 30 days.

The Apple Takes Root

Robert Prince established the first commercial apple nursery in 1737 at his famous Prince Nursery in Flushing, New York, supplying tree cuttings to gardeners and small commercial growers until the apple's successful mid-nineteenth-century entry into the national commercial market. The German immigrant son of a viticulturist, George Ellwanger—along with a partner, an Irish immigrant named Patrick Barry who had worked at the Prince Nursery in Flushing—established in 1840 the seven-acre Mount Hope Nursery in Rochester. The nursery's location was strategic: It stood right next to the Erie Canal, giving the partners a shipping advantage of more than a week over East Coast nurseries seeking to service Central and Western New York as well as the Midwest. Ellwanger and Barry went around the continent to gather specimens and to show their stock. While the partners considered the pear a most elegant fruit, the apple gained prominence in Western New York and its success was reflected at the nursery. In 1843, a Mount Hope Nursery catalog listed twenty-nine varieties of pears and ninety-four varieties of apples available for sale, including Baldwin, Greening, and Jonathan apples. In 1848, along with a number of other fruits, Barry took the Northern Spy apple to exhibit overseas; this variety was discovered just south of Rochester in 1800. By 1855, Mount Hope Nursery had expanded to four hundred acres. That year, Barry spearheaded the Fruit Growers Society of Western New York (it ultimately became the New York Horticultural Society).

Within fifteen more years, the nursery added another 250 acres, making it the largest plant nursery in the nineteenth century. Mount Hope Nursery became so important that Rochester began to be known as the Flower City instead of the Flour City. Flowers notwithstanding, fruit orchards were the reason for the nursery's need for more acreage—450 of the 650 acres were in fruit trees, with emphasis on the pear but especially on the apple.

Overall demand for fresh fruit tripled across the country between 1850 and 1900. Orchard fruits were at the forefront of this demand, with the apple in the lead. By the end of the century, New York apples and other tree fruits surpassed the commercial success of Doolittle's black raspberry bushes. Horticulturists have speculated that the apple's rise may have been because it blooms later in spring than many other fruits, a trait quite suitable to northern climates where spring frost is a threat. In any case, by the turn of the century many Western and Central New York farmers had clearly added fruit to their farm income (in addition to cultivated fruit, a small commercial English walnut industry took root around Keuka and Canandaigua Lakes). The top apple-producing Western New York locations were Niagara, Orleans, Monroe, and Wayne counties. Bordering the southern shore of Lake Ontario, Wayne was the largest apple-producing county of them all.

Across New York, at least five hundred apple varieties had been identified by the turn of the century. Ontario, Onondaga, and Yates counties numbered among the important counties where new varieties were being developed (in the Finger Lakes region, the Baldwin variety was king). By this time, the apple represented more than 50 percent of the state's orchard fruits, and more than 80 percent of the commercial bushels of fruits produced in New York. That year, Wayne County boasted twenty-one thousand acres of apple orchards, representing nearly thirty-four acres of apple trees per square mile. The county produced the greatest number of dried and evaporated apple products in the United States, during a time when Western New York (with help from Central New York) accounted for one-fourth of all commercial apple production in the country. Most of the apple orchards ran along the 125-mile stretch from Niagara Falls east along Lake Ontario and extended about 10 miles south of the lake's shores into the Genesee Valley and the northern areas of Canandaigua, Keuka, Seneca, Cayuga, Skaneateles, and Owasco lakes.

In the first decade of the twentieth century, the order of importance of apple acreage in Finger Lakes counties was Wayne, Monroe, Genesee, Ontario, Yates, Seneca, and, on the western fringe of the region, Livingston. Commercial apple tree cultivation seemed to do best on the drumlins at between three hundred and eight hundred feet above sea level. Rooted in stony loam, apple trees fared well on an easterly slope that would protect them from the region's strong westerly storm winds. The same Lake Ontario influence spawned a commercial peach industry that, although it never rose to the prominence of the apple, flourished in the region nonetheless. Pears reached commercial importance about equal to peaches. The region for pear cultivation extended farther south from Lake Ontario, where less hospitable clay soils were situated, and where drainage was not as important to that crop as it was to apples. In the early twentieth century, the region began to slowly support commercial cherries, too, and Geneva soon became the center of a cherry-canning industry. Finally, commercial red raspberries replaced the black raspberry industry, especially near and west of Seneca Lake. Finger Lakes fruit production was key in making New York the top state in canned and dried fruits, which of course included the apple.

When commercial apple farming began in the Finger Lakes region, sheep pasturing was the valuable way of "treating" the soil around fruit trees; hogs had to be moved away from the trees so that they would not damage them. According to U. P. Hedrick, Geneva Agricultural Experiment Station bulletins in the 1880s were solely responsible for establishing better fertilizing methods in the region. Other than the natural droppings of pastured livestock around orchards, Hedrick found that farmers believed adding fertilizer would overburden trees, causing them to produce too much fruit, which would weaken them. For that matter, spraying for insect and fungus control was not much favored, either. In the early twentieth century, consumer demand was unaffected by "imperfect" fruit. Spraying became widespread only after scientists at agricultural stations across the country proved to farmers that sprayed trees produced a greater number of attractive fruits and consequently more revenue.

Hedrick also claimed that before extension agency bulletins, pruning apple trees was frowned upon. He named one particular nineteenth-century horticulturist, Thomas Meehan, who wrote in 1868 that pruning stunted tree growth. He believed that apple trees needed to be raised tall so that livestock grazing nearby could not eat the valuable fruit.

Farmers interested in starting a commercial apple orchard couldn't, and didn't, give up other means of support. They had to wait a number of years for trees to mature and produce a viable crop. After that first crop, however, the investment in an apple orchard could pay off over four or five decades, and that's what made it an appealing business. Still, up to 25 percent of apple orchards were operated on the share system, where a renter took care of the orchard and gave shares of the crop to the landowner. The system produced a few problems, not the least of which was that a number of landowners got burned by renters who lost interest in taking care of the orchards during those first few years when the trees did not produce. In 1896, at the end of a downturn in apple prices, landowner farmers made up the majority of Western New York apple orchards, contributing heavily to the state's overall fifty-four million harvested apple bushels.

Despite its apparent promise of success, apple farming did not replace other crops, and that was a major strength of the region. Apple prices began to come back up by 1910, but western and even southern states had entered into the commercial apple market and proved formidable competition. The farm economy in Western New York managed to compete and retain its apple industry precisely because farmers relied on a number of other cash crops alongside fruit; the fact that the region had ready access to the largest population density in the country serviced by an efficient nearby rail system also played a major role.

The biggest drawbacks in Finger Lakes apple production were humidity in summer and erratic weather that produced severe temperature swings in winter, which could kill off the buds for that year's crop. Because farmers relied on more than just apple crops, care of the trees was not as much a priority as in other US locations where the apple began to drive the local economy. In addition, the Baldwin, which led apple production, was prolific but not top-quality; that was the reason for its use, in Wayne County, primarily for dried apple products.

Apple prices were on the rise in the early 1900s, but the few years of low prices at the end of the previous century had a lasting effect. In 1918, New York produced just six million barrels (about twenty million bushels) of apples, two-thirds of which were produced in the Lake Ontario fruit belt. This was a drop in production from a decade earlier of about 50 percent. Also, two decades into the twentieth century, the nearly century-old Lake Ontario belt commercial apple orchards had aged and were not being replaced. In their 1921 book *The Commercial Apple Industry of North America*, J.C. Folger and S.M. Thomson wondered what would become of the Lake Ontario apple industry if new orchard plantings did not go forward soon.

In 1915, in an attempt to provide better-quality eating apples, Cornell's Experiment Station released its first hybrid, the Cortland, to great success. Eight and nine years later, Cornell released the Macoun and the Lodi varieties, respectively. The single most important development promoted by Cornell scientists came in the late 1930s and early '40s, when bulletins explained to the commercial apple industry the benefit of Controlled Atmospheric Storage (CAS).

Controlled Atmospheric Storage

Apple cold storage was an ancient concept rediscovered in the early 1800s by a Frenchman, Jacques Bérard. CAS was an improvement over cold storage. Simply put, CAS is a means to control oxygen, carbon dioxide, nitrogen concentrations, temperature, and humidity in a sealed, regulated environment so that apples harvested in the fall can be sold all year round. The practice was in wide use in England around the time that Cornell promoted its use in New York.

CAS was a perfect fit for large-scale cooperative packing, storing, and ultimately shipping to market, but Finger Lakes apple growers had yet to discover the benefit of cooperative marketing and communal processing. In other parts of the country, during harvest season trucks went from farm to farm to pick up bushels and take them to the communal packing and storage house. In Western New York, the most prevalent system of marketing apples was for cash buyers to offer a price for an entire crop in advance. The buyer was responsible for sorting and packing. This situation held true even in the large Wayne County dried apple portion of the industry. Rather than send the crop to a large commercial drying facility, most of the drying was done on hundreds of individual farms using evaporators or distillation devices and kilns.

On the other hand, apples intended for canning or for cider were sent to large operations in places like Geneva, where fruit canning was centered. To get the apples there, farmers cooperated by loading their crops onto trucks that went from farm to farm to pick up fruits and either deliver them to a railroad station like the one at Rochester, or transport them directly to Geneva.

In October 1931, the Mohawk Valley's Beech-Nut Company patented the first commercial vacuum jar. Not long thereafter, when the company released the first widely distributed baby food in a jar, Western New York apples enjoyed a successful market almost on their doorstep. Still, competition loomed, from the Midwest and especially from the West Coast.

Washington State was threatening to ship apples to states whose markets had been available to New York apple growers of earlier generations. In response, New York State apple growers joined in 1935 with New England growers to form the New York and New England Apple Institute, a promotion arm of the industry. The New York contingent was largely made up of Hudson Valley apple growers. In Western New York, growers formed the New York Apple Growers Association in 1950 to address fluctuating prices as well as the outlook for the future. Per capita apple consumption in the United States averaged thirty pounds per year in the 1950s, and New York had slipped to second in production behind Washington. Recognizing the threat, New York apple growers pressed for a government-sponsored marketing order, which came to fruition in 1959.

Going into the 1960s, apples accounted for nearly 60 percent of all New York fruit and nut sales. Wayne County accounted for about one-third of the apples produced in the nine apple-producing counties of New York. In 1964, however, New York apple production was just one million bushels greater than the production recorded for 1918. Luckily, even though apple production seemed stagnant, the Northeast market was large enough to take all the apples that New York growers produced: While the country on the whole consumed thirty pounds per capita annually, population growth in the Northeast had created an eastern market per capita consumption that neared forty pounds. The Lake Ontario apple district was here to stay.

5

The Grape

Wine is the most healthful and most hygienic
of beverages.

—Louis Pasteur

GRAPEVINES PREDATE HUMANITY, but grapevine
cultivation is believed to have begun about eight
thousand years ago, about the time of the first agrarian
civilization in Mesopotamia (the Near East). How grape
cultivation began remains a subject for speculation, but
here's one possibility.

Wild grapevines spread their tendrils, producing
more and more wood as they travel along the ground or
up the trunks of other plants. Nature assigns wild vines
either a male or a female role, which means that pollina-
tion requires the right weather and bee conditions. The
process is haphazard and unreliable, not good enough
to count on a consistent grape crop from year to year,
and certainly not good enough to establish a commercial
grape-based business. Often, however, nature produces a
few freaks. In the case of grapevines, those freaks would
be hermaphroditic vines with male and female flowers,
which are capable of producing fruit more consistently.
Perhaps an astute Mesopotamian farmer noticed this difference and began selecting the consistent vines to plant.
That same farmer may have also noticed that if he cut
back the wood annually, the grapevine produced larger
and more abundant fruit. If so, he may have been the
first to cultivate grapevines to make wine.

Chardonnay grapes of the Finger Lakes region.
Courtesy VisitFingerLakes.com.

Records show that the Vikings, the first to explore the northeastern portion of North America, mentioned the abundant wild grapes they saw. Later explorers observed the wild vines, too; some wrote about their powerful, acrid taste. Records also show that the Iroquois ate grapes. No records have surfaced revealing that either the earliest explorers or the Iroquois purposely produced wine in New York.

Grape harvest in a Finger Lakes vineyard.
Courtesy VisitFingerLakes.com.

Still, wine had great spiritual and commercial importance in the Old World. That's why settlers and colonists in the New World tried to harness the local grapes to produce wine, but they were never satisfied with the results. Rather than the sought-after subtlety of wines they remembered from home, the first European settlers in the South and Southeast on the North American continent faced forward, grapey wines with extremely high acidity that they found offensive. They turned to what they knew: They imported grapevines from Europe.

Seventeenth-century Dutch colonists were the first to try to grow European vines in New York State. They began approximately near today's New Utrecht Avenue in Brooklyn—they failed. Later, eighteenth- and nineteenth-century attempts also failed in Brooklyn, in and close to what is Prospect Park, as well as farther away in Long Island. The European vines imported for these attempts lasted two to three years before they simply shriveled and died. This pattern of failure in New York was a continuation of the failure in southern and southeastern colonies. The colonists did not understand that while all wine grapes are of the *Vitis* genus, Old and New World grapevines

Homemade Wine

What differentiates red from white wine is that the former is fermented with skins intact and then pressed as wine; the latter is pressed first and fermented as juice. For the purpose of ease, the following recipe is for white wine.

Ingredients and Equipment

From a home winemaker supply shop secure 6 gallons of your favorite grape juice, a packet of yeast recommended by the proprietor (plus some sugar to add if you need more for the alcohol volume that you want), two 5-gallon carboys plus two 1-gallon jugs (have one carboy filled with 4 ½ gallons of juice and each jug filled with ¾ gallon), some cheesecloth, tubing, two bungs and two air locks, a hand corking device, 24 wine bottles (750 milliliter size), and corks.

Note: The winemaker shop proprietor will recommend adding sulfur dioxide powder to protect the wine from oxidizing. Take the recommendation and follow the instructions religiously or you run the risk of ruining the wine.

You'll also need a clean, cool location for storage after fermentation, or a refrigerator.

Directions

1. Sterilize everything.
2. Add the yeast and any sugar needed according to instructions from the winemaking shop.
3. Cover the carboy and jug openings with cheesecloth.
4. Keep the juice at room temperature. Fermentation should begin within a day or so—and it can erupt violently, which is why you don't fill the carboy and jugs all the way, and you cover them with cheesecloth. After a few days, the fermentation will mellow; insert the bungs, fill the air locks midway with water, and insert them into the bungs.
5. Watch the bubbling air locks daily to keep the water at mid-level.
6. When the water in the air locks ceases to bubble, the fermentation is at its end; this could take days or it could take weeks, depending on temperature, but do not let it get hot.
7. When fermentation ends, follow the instructions for the sulfur dioxide addition and then insert the tube into the carboy until it reaches the sediment at the bottom—do not insert it into the sediment.
8. Siphon the new wine into a clean carboy that is set well below the first so that you get a smooth, finished flow; top up the carboy with the wine from the jugs, tilting them so that the sediment remains in the bottles.
9. Either refrigerate or store the carboy in a very cool place.
10. Over the next 6 months, siphon the wine from one carboy to the next three times, being careful to keep it a smooth flow, and follow the recommended sulfur dioxide regimen.
11. In the spring, bottle and cork the wine.

belong to separate species. The northeastern region of North America was home to the *aestivalis, riparia, labrusca,* and *vulpina* species; in Europe, the species is *vinifera*. Each species had adapted to its primary environment.

Courtesy VisitFingerLakes.com.

A Perfect Home

It comes as no surprise that wild grapevines flourished in the temperate Northeast; the region provides an ample growing season as well as the necessary dormant season for vines to revitalize. In the Finger Lakes, land and climate conspire to create perfect conditions for wine grapes. Certainly, the climate between November and March provides incentive

for plants to take a much-needed rest, to regenerate the energy necessary for spring budding and flowering. The Finger Lakes growing season
between April and October is long enough, with average temperatures
warm and sunny enough, for healthy grapevine growth. The region's

cool summer nights counteract the heat of the sun, preventing grapes
from overmaturing into a sweet mass of uninteresting flabbiness, maintaining their natural crispness to serve as a wine's backbone. The gentle
slopes of the region are important, too, as they provide good air and
water drainage through vineyards. Of all the attributes of the Finger
Lakes region, the critical one may be the fog of warmer air that rises
from the lakes up the steep slopes during harvest, when autumn air
temperature is cooler than the lake's water. As it dissipates slowly up

Vineyards, Ontario
County, NY.
*Courtesy
VisitFingerLakes.com.*

A Finger Lakes vineyard in winter. Courtesy *VisitFingerLakes.com*.

the slopes, the warm fog protects vineyards from potential early frosts during the time when grapes have just a short window of opportunity to mature.

To be sure, none of this was known four centuries ago in North America, probably because grapevines were wild and abundant enough that no one thought about ways to harness the spreading tendrils. For successive millennia after the first humans set foot in North America, no wine from grapes was produced commercially. Wine was produced in the southwestern and western portions of the continent by the seventeenth century, but even there, it was mainly for spiritual and communal use. Commercial wine production success arguably arrived in the late 1820s, after a lawyer and financier named Nicholas Longworth established a winery in Cincinnati, Ohio. Longworth's success was the result of a winemaking mistake that created the first North American commercial sparkling wine. His success spawned further commercial interest in the Midwest, and the establishment of commercial wineries in New York wasn't far behind.

Growing Consistent Grape Varieties

Scientists know that grapevine species differ between the Eurasian and North American landscape, but rarely do separate grape varieties prove to be the originals. Over millennia, grapevine seeds intermingled in the field, regularly producing new varieties. For that reason, planting seeds for commercial wine growing is problematic: As with any other cultivated fruit, you never know which grape variety will result from a seed. The only way to plant and get the grape variety that you want is to graft the scion wood of that variety onto a rootstock so that what grows above the graft is what you choose to grow and what grows below the graft and in the ground is a root system suitable for that earth.

Because of its proximity to New York City, the Hudson Valley became home to the first successful commercial wine industry in New York State—small as it was. Wherever they had been produced, upstate or down, in the nineteenth century commercial New York wines were based neither on European nor on American wild vines. Rather, the majority of the wines were based on a few newly discovered grapevines that were the result of spontaneous crossings in the field between the unsuccessful European and American grapevine species. The new field hybrid vines took on some—but not all—of the taste profile of the European grapes. More important, the field crosses survived their New World environment. At first, however, their field cross status was not known; they were simply considered native vines. It took lab work much later in history to uncover their pedigree. The two most prominent grapevines of the period were Catawba (the grape that launched Longworth's sparkling wine success in Ohio) and Isabella. Each grape variety is believed to have originated in the Carolinas. Henry Wadsworth Longfellow apparently adored Catawba. In 1854, he wrote an ode to it:

This song of mine
Is a Song of the Vine,
To be sung by the glowing embers
Of wayside inns,
When the rain begins
To darken the drear Novembers.

It is not a song
Of the Scuppernong,
From warm Carolinian valleys,
Nor the Isabel
And the Muscadel
That bask in our garden alleys.

Nor the red Mustang,
Whose clusters hang
O'er the waves of the Colorado,
And the fiery flood
Of whose purple blood
Has a dash of Spanish bravado.

For richest and best
Is the wine of the West,
That grows by the Beautiful River;
Whose sweet perfume
Fills all the room
With a benison on the giver.

And as hollow trees
Are the haunts of bees,
Forever going and coming;

So this crystal hive
Is all alive
With a swarming and buzzing and humming.

Very good in its way
Is the Verzenay,
Or the Sillery soft and creamy;
But Catawba wine
Has a taste more divine,
More dulcet, delicious, and dreamy.

There grows no vine
By the haunted Rhine,
By Danube or Guadalquivir,
Nor on island or cape,
That bears such a grape
As grows by the Beautiful River.

Drugged is their juice
For foreign use,
When shipped o'er the reeling Atlantic,
To rack our brains
With the fever pains,
That have driven the Old World frantic.

To the sewers and sinks
With all such drinks,
And after them tumble the mixer;
For a poison malign
Is such Borgia wine,
Or at best but a Devil's Elixir.

While pure as a spring

Is the wine I sing,

And to praise it, one needs but name it;

For Catawba wine

Has need of no sign,

No tavern-bush to proclaim it.

And this Song of the Vine,

This greeting of mine,

The winds and the birds shall deliver

To the Queen of the West,

In her garlands dressed,

On the banks of the Beautiful River.

Longfellow wrote the poem in praise of Nicholas Longworth's sparkling Catawba wine of Cincinnati, Ohio. The name Ohio was derived from an Iroquois word meaning "beautiful river."

Grapes for the Table

As grapes and wine made their way into the Midwest and Northeast, the southern portion of the old Pulteney Estate south of Keuka Lake was in an economic depression. Timber resources of the Pleasant Valley were diminishing; what remained was re-routed from the arduous and expensive journey south down the Susquehanna to the faster and less costly waterway systems to the north that emptied into the Erie Canal. Other than businessmen who had earlier built their small empires, most farmers were ill equipped to get their timber to market. Rounding out their economic problems was what a number of nineteenth- and early-twentieth-century writers described as a "famine" that struck the overall southern tier of the Finger Lakes region, the result of an apparent severe drought.

This was the situation in 1829 when the Reverend William W. Bostwick, descendant of one of the seventeen families that settled Connecticut, arrived in the small village of Hammondsport at the southern tip of Keuka Lake.

Pegtown

In the late 18th century, a few Revolutionary War veterans worked their way through the Pleasant Valley to the lakeshore where they settled Pegtown, a reference to the shoe industry that flourished there. Around the time of the Erie Canal construction, Pegtown was renamed Hammondsport to honor Judge Hammond, instrumental in forwarding the project to dig the canal that connected Keuka and Seneca lakes.

Bostwick went to Hammondsport to establish a congregation. There he built the Saint James Episcopal Church, which still stands in the village today. The reverend was also a gardener with a wide interest in horticulture, including grapes. He probably aspired to produce wine for sacramental purposes, but no evidence has surfaced that he made wine at all. The evidence that he grew grapes comes from the reverend himself, in articles that he wrote in 1833 for the *Genesee Farmer and Gardener's Journal*. The highly regarded Journal was the first farm periodical published in New York State, in Rochester beginning in 1831.

It isn't clear if Bostwick considered the field-hybrid Catawba and Isabella cuttings that he bought from an associate in the Hudson Valley to be strictly native, but his articles clearly indicate that he thought of them as a source for making wine. He saw the future relying on "the improving of our native varieties." He was quite sure that one day a purposeful marriage of European and Native American vines would produce palatable, profitable wine. More than a century would pass before Finger Lakes vineyards would reflect the reverend's hybridizing dream.

Around the time of Bostwick's vineyard planting, another reverend, Samuel Warren, planted vines in Livingston County, on the western edge of the Finger Lakes region. Warren's purpose was expressly to produce wine for sacramental and medicinal purposes, which he accomplished and marketed in 1836, three years before the commercial wine success in the Hudson Valley (the legacy of that success is today's Brotherhood Winery). Warren's family winery lasted nearly forty years, until eminent domain forced the family to give way to railroad tracks. In all that time, the Warren family's wine distribution didn't seem to exceed their western Finger Lakes boundary.

At Keuka Lake, Reverend Bostwick's cuttings became the catalyst for a table grape industry. By the 1830s, hundreds of acres of vineyards for table grapes had been planted where trees used to stand in the Pleasant Valley. Grape farms spread quickly to Hammondsport and up the slopes on the west side of Keuka Lake, where grapes were grown on local farms, handpicked, and delivered to one of three ports on the lake: at Branchport in the town of Jerusalem at the north end of the west branch of the lake's *Y* configuration, at Gibson's Landing in the town of Pulteney about midway on the west side of the lake, and at Snug Harbor just northwest of Hammondsport. From there the

grapes went to Hammondsport, where they were packed at Grimley's Grape Packing House and loaded on steamships for the journey north in the direction of Penn Yan at the tip of the lake's east branch, or on a stagecoach to make their way south to Bath and surrounding communities.

Sending grapes long distances was not an easy task. The first of these shipments took place in 1847, from Keuka Lake along the Erie Canal system and on to New York City. The cost of shipping and the perishable nature of the fruit conspired against Lemuel Hastings, the grape farmer who lost money on the venture. Only when the Erie Railroad line was up and running through Bath in 1852 was the stage set for the Keuka table grape industry to successfully grow beyond local boundaries. That event came around 1856 when Josiah Prentiss, a farmer in Pulteney, packed a ton of Isabella grapes in half barrels so securely that they were not damaged on their way to New York City. The sixteen cents a pound that Prentiss grossed on the shipment represented the first major profit in Keuka grapes.

A vineyard is sensitive to weather anomalies, but not as sensitive as many other cash crops. The opportunity that table grapes represented spread from Keuka to nearby Seneca Lake and into what was becoming an internationally known table grape industry. The market for fresh

The Susquehanna River, the main transportation waterway before the Erie Canal was built.
Courtesy Chris Houston.

Finger Lakes table grapes remained strong into the early part of the twentieth century, but by mid-century East Coast grape producers found it difficult to compete with West Coast grapes, where the climate made it cheaper to produce them abundantly and ship them across the country. According to a government chart, between 1923 and 1943 Finger Lakes grape shipments across the nation dropped from a high of 5,641 carloads in 1924 to a low of 16 carloads in 1943.

Early on, the market for Western New York grape juice was strong. After Louis Pasteur's mid-nineteenth-century discovery of the secret to beverage contamination and how to fix it by heating and then cooling, physician and dentist Thomas Bramwell Welch began producing in 1869 Dr. Welch's Unfermented Wine. Welch was in favor of temperance, and so he set up his operation in the reputed temperance town of Vineland, New Jersey, and used locally grown grapes for his pasteurized grape juice product. In 1893 he and his son Charles established the Welch's Grape Juice Company in Westfield, New York, situated in Lake Erie country. As Welch's expanded during the early twentieth century, vineyard acreage in Western New York grew rapidly to supply the company that even reached into the Finger Lakes to buy grapes.

A growing anti-alcohol sentiment in the United States at the time notwithstanding, and with flourishing grape juice production, the population of European immigrants in New York guaranteed that wine production would take place in the state. The Finger Lakes region was no exception.

Grapes for Juice and Wine

Trained as a viticulturist in Germany, Andrew Risinger (also spelled Reisinger) brought that knowledge with him when he emigrated from Europe to New York. In 1854, he planted a vineyard in Pulteney. Risinger introduced to the Finger Lakes region the importance of proper vineyard site selection, plus new methods of trellising, training, and pruning vines. There's evidence that he was behind much of the success of vineyards that went into the Pleasant Valley; there's also evidence that he produced wine from local grapes but was at first unimpressed with the result. Apparently, Risinger and Josiah Prentiss were neighbors. It's possible that Risinger taught his neighbor how to grow the table grapes that Prentiss had sold in New York City in 1856. It's also possible that Risinger helped his neighbor, in 1857, when Prentiss sent to an agent in New York City the first known shipment of commercial wines from Keuka Lake. Produced from Catawba and Isabella grapes, the wines made a profit for Prentiss. Still, for whatever reason, the Risinger/Prentiss foray into wine production was short-lived, though the dream of winemaking at Keuka Lake did not die.

The year following Prentiss's brief success with commercial wine, Grattan H. Wheeler and two of his sons opened the Wheeler Wine Cellar about a mile south of Hammondsport, in the heart of the Pleasant Valley. For the next two years, the Wheelers sold their wine locally amid a stir of talk about the possibility of future world renown for a Keuka Lake wine industry. That future arrived in 1860, when Charles D. Champlin organized a dozen men to help him form the Hammondsport and Pleasant Valley

Urbana Wine Company building in the late 19th century, the first commercial winery in the Finger Lakes.
Courtesy Yates County History Center.

Wine Company (the word Hammondsport was later dropped from the name). The winery was built just south of the Wheeler's winery in the Pleasant Valley. The article of association concerning wine production at the Pleasant Valley Wine Company was quite specific: "to produce native wines."

With those four words, a commercially successful Finger Lakes wine industry began.

The Pleasant Valley Wine Company was off to a splendid start. In its first year, the company shelled out seventeen hundred dollars to buy twenty tons of grapes from Keuka growers, which included over a ton from Josiah Prentiss. The company's winemaker, a German immigrant named Weber, turned that into four thousand gallons of wine; this was followed in the second year with more than five thousand gallons. By 1862, Grattan Wheeler had abandoned his family winery to become president at the Pleasant Valley Wine Company. That year, the winery received the first U S bonded license issued by the Treasury Department as a means to tax alcohol in order to help fund what the federal government knew was coming: war with the South. By the time the war ended, the winery had increased its production to fifty thousand gallons. A few years after that, the company added the Masson brothers, Joseph and Jules, to its staff, the team responsible for the sparkling Catawba wine produced by Nicholas Longworth's winery in Cincinnati. Charles Champlin wanted the Masson brothers to produce world-class sparkling wine under the Pleasant Valley label.

It is to be regretted that the hard-earned experience of others is not taken as a guide, but the fact will be learned, sooner or later, that east of the range of the Rocky Mountains no climate has yet been found suitable for the continued healthy growth of the foreign grape.

—*The American Report of the Commissioner of Agriculture,* 1868

The commissioner's view did not address what would happen should American vines be sent to Europe. When viticulturists in the Old World became interested in New World grape varieties, American vines were sent over for test planting. Then, at around the time of the American Civil War, some vines in France seemed to mimic the European vines that had died a couple of years after they were introduced to North America. It turned out that, while climate was part of the problem for the transplanted vines, a near-microscopic pale yellow root louse named *Phylloxera vastatrix* that lived on American grapevine roots was the real culprit. The many grapevine species of North America had learned to accommodate the root louse, but the European vinifera grapevine species had no resistance to it. When American vines were introduced into European vineyards, the root louse spread through the soil and attacked the non-resistant vines of Europe. When that happened, disaster followed.

Over the next two decades, the *Phylloxera* blight nearly wiped out vineyard appellations throughout the European continent. During that time, many attempts to address the problem were tried and abandoned until, in the latter part of the nineteenth century, scientists discovered that resistance to the root louse was established when *vinifera* scion wood was grafted onto rootstock cuttings from the American vine species. Like grafted fruit trees, above the graft grows the fruit that you seek; below it is the root system that produces best in a particular soil and location. Grafting could not be done onto rootstocks from grapes like Catawba or Isabella because, as spontaneous field hybrids, they had European blood running through them that made them susceptible to

Phylloxera. For grafting to succeed, the rootstock had to be truly wild *Phylloxera*-resistant North American vines.

A major project was developed to catalog and send hundreds of different rootstocks to Europe for a grafting program. Thomas Munson, a horticulturist with extensive grapevine knowledge, oversaw the project from his base in Denison, Texas. His supervision is why the state of Texas today hosts the greatest number of grapevine species and grape varieties in the United States. The vines sent to Munson were from the US South, Midwest, and Northeast, as well as from Canada.

The practice of grafting European vines onto North American root-stock continues today as the only effective way to prevent a *Phylloxera* outbreak anywhere in the world.

Success at Home

The Pleasant Valley Wine Company lived up to Charles Champlin's dream with its first sparkling wine release in 1870. Proud of the Masson brothers' effort, Champlin sent some wine to the famous Palmer House Hotel in Boston so that his friend Marshall P. Wilder, founder of the American Pomological and US Agriculture Societies, could serve the wine at a dinner he was hosting. Wilder's dinner guests dubbed the wine "the greatest champagne in the entire western continent," providing in 1871 a name for the first national Finger Lakes wine brand: Great Western Champagne. The brand went on to capture a number of awards in the 1870s, in America and—despite its overall makeup of the American "native" Catawba grape—in Europe, too.

At the end of the Civil War, another group of investors at Keuka Lake raised two hundred thousand dollars to form the Urbana Wine Company. The facility was built about three miles north of Hammondsport, along the western lakeshore. It was a spectacular building; its steeple-like roof made it the tallest of any in the area, and its loading and unloading dock could handle large volumes of shipments. Urbana's owners had grand plans. The winery's express purpose was to produce sparkling wine that would compete with its neighbor the Pleasant Valley Wine Company as well as far-off competitors in France. For that reason, from its beginning Urbana's chief winemakers were always recruited from France's Champagne region. The winery ran into some trouble in 1890 and went bankrupt, but in the following year, more money was raised and the winery began a successful run that ended in 1985. For most

Honeoye Lake, one of the smaller lakes in the western region of the Finger Lakes. *Courtesy VisitFingerLakes.com.*

of its more than one hundred years, the winery did business under the name of its well-known successful brand, Gold Seal.

Toward the end of the 1870s, Keuka Lake was home to no fewer than sixteen wineries.

In 1880, Walter Taylor and his father, a cooper from Tioga County in the southern tier, started the Taylor Company on the west side of Keuka Lake; it was situated on the Bully Hill three miles north of Hammondsport and about two thousand feet above sea level. The hill got its name in the days when rowdy young men from the area went down the hill to the tavern in Pulteney on Saturday nights and bullied the locals into fights.

At first, the Taylor Company produced grape juice. By 1882, father and son were the proud owners of Bonded Winery License #17, and they changed the company name to the Taylor Wine and Grape Juice Company. The Taylor family business doggedly grew each year by establishing loyalty and trust with local grape growers, whom the Taylors came to rely on as their business expanded. Their facility had no electricity; production was controlled by either steam power or the force of gravity, and the Taylors thus had no bottling line. Taylor wines and juices were sold in their own constructed cooperage, usually in thirty-gallon capacity. In the retail shop, customers brought their own receptacles into which wine was drawn from the barrels.

More vineyards and wineries were added in the 1880s and '90s at Keuka Lake in Steuben County, at Honeoye and Canandaigua lakes in Ontario County, around the village of Penn Yan, and at Seneca Lake in Yates County, but Steuben County accounted for more than 50 percent of the region's grape and wine production. By the turn of the century, Hammondsport in Steuben County had become the center of the Finger Lakes wine industry. Grape juice, wine, and to a lesser extent table grapes supported hundreds of Keuka Lake area farming families. Nearly 150 years ago, good vineyard land around Keuka was valued between five hundred and a thousand dollars per acre (from eleven to twenty-three thousand in today's dollars). Grapes also supported a number of ancillary industries: basket and box production; wire making; cooperage; mills to cut vineyard posts; small tools; blacksmithing; local shops and grocers to supply a growing populace that was fed by dozens of produce and livestock farms. In addition, motorcycles and naval aeronautics, developed after the turn of the century by Hammondsport native Glenn H. Curtiss, supported the community with good manufacturing and sales jobs. Its natural beauty turned Keuka Lake into a major vacation and tourist location, too, with hotels, restaurants, and theatrical venues. Hammondsport and Pulteney were self-contained communities, where a person could get anything necessary either for survival or for entertainment.

At the same time that grapes and wine brought prosperity in the nineteenth century, another product of Western and Central New York took form: a gestating social movement that posed an existential threat to the wine industry in the twentieth century.

Temperance; n: self-restraint in the face of temptation or desire.

Prohibition; n: the act or process of forbidding something.

A women's rights convention of 1848 in Seneca Falls, a town situated between and just north of Seneca and Cayuga lakes, brought native New Yorker and avid abolitionist Elizabeth Cady Stanton together with the Massachusetts-born abolitionist Susan B. Anthony. The two became major local drivers of a nascent women's suffrage movement. Later, the Rochester-born educator Francis Willard presided over the Woman's Christian Temperance Union out of Erie County in Western New York, which she then aligned with the Prohibition Party, the nation's third major political party. By the turn of the century, seeking political power as potent as the anti-alcohol movement had gained, the New York women's suffrage movement aligned with the prohibition forces.

Coupled with the fervor of famous anti-alcohol people like the preacher Billy Sunday and three-time losing presidential candidate William Jennings Bryan, the anti-alcohol movement gained momentum because its proponents made a good point. The young United States was a hard-drinking country. There was always hard apple cider, but New York grapes also joined pears to produce the equally important brandy—between 1862 and 1865, the Pleasant Valley Wine Company produced sixty-two thousand gallons of it. New York's hops growers were also kept busy supplying all the breweries located in just about every one of the original settlements that had grown into populated towns and villages. The result of all this alcohol was the widespread establishment of saloons, the primary target of the anti-alcohol movement (one historical reference claimed that in the early years of the nineteenth century, there were fourteen thousand saloons in the nation, which, based on the population at the time, leads to the incredible estimate of one saloon for approximately every two hundred adult men). That the saloons served alcohol was only one of the problems the women's movement addressed. Saloons were places for gambling and prostitution, often leaving the family breadwinner drunk and broke, and the family destitute.

At first, and for quite some time, Finger Lakes wine producers were not convinced that wine, the product of moderation, was part of the anti-alcohol message. By the turn of the century, local newspapers were not so sanguine. The editor of the *Hammondsport Herald* ran many warnings in the newspaper, calling for more production and promotion of grape juice as a way to keep grape farmers solvent on the day that prohibition legislation was to arrive. The anti-alcohol Welch's Grape Juice owners competed for Finger Lakes grapes, and the company went into a decided effort to sign up grape growers for juice production.

Yet despite the ominous signs and the warnings of newspaper editors, the Finger Lakes wine industry continued to grow.

The California Threat

West Coast commercial wineries began about a decade before the Hammondsport wine industry. California winemakers had a distinct table wine edge, as their environment proved suitable for European grapevines. In 1912, in a display of hope for the future of East Coast wine, U. P. Hedrick at the Geneva Experiment Station announced that the horticultural department had reached positive results in a program to develop new grape varieties by joining European grapevines with their North American counterparts. It was the beginning of official efforts to come up with grape varieties in the Northeast to produce table wines with the subtlety of European wines to compete with California.

While grape research picked up at the agricultural station in Geneva, the call for temperance had shifted to a call for outright prohibition. In 1912, a number of states enacted alcohol prohibition laws. Soon after that, the First World War gave prohibitionists a chance to use nationalism in their war against alcohol; they attacked the many breweries owned by German immigrants. When the United States finally entered the war in 1917, Congress passed a law that banned distilled spirits production during wartime. The ban was the death knell for spirits distillation in the Finger Lakes, and it set the stage for a national prohibition on production and distribution of all alcoholic beverages, which was in fact soon passed in Washington. After a full year of state-to-state ratification of the Eighteenth Amendment to the US Constitution, national Prohibition of the sale and distribution of beverage alcohol began in January 1920. Stories are told of people crowding Hammondsport in late December carrying all manner of containers to fill up before the wineries closed.

Finger Lakes grape farmers at the very least still had a market for juice and a lesser one for table grapes. Hops growers were not so fortunate. At the turn of the century, blight had wiped out large swaths of Central New York's hops. Prohibition struck the final blow both to hops farming and to the malting houses.

A number of Finger Lakes wineries had the resources and the will to press on. They took advantage of loopholes in Prohibition legislation that allowed the production and distribution of sacramental and medicinal wine as well as wine for cooking (Campbell's Soup was a Prohibition-era customer for Finger Lakes sherry wines). Another loophole in the legislation guaranteed that the head of a household could produce up to two hundred gallons of wine per year for home use. This loophole was instrumental in catapulting the Taylor family's business into national prominence.

In 1917, the Taylor Wine and Grape Juice Company was still located about three miles north of Hammondsport in a facility that had no electricity. That year, the Taylor family bought the Columbia Wine Company situated in the Pleasant Valley just a few hundred feet south of the Pleasant Valley Wine Company. Invested in the local electric company, Columbia's owner had electrified the winery and installed an especially well-equipped bottling line. The Taylor family planned to put this to good use during Prohibition. After changing the company name to the Taylor Grape Juice Company, this time adding mention on the label that it was the same company that used to produce wine, the Taylors produced the first-ever local grape juice in bottles alongside their usual offering of juice in thirty-gallon kegs. With the juices came a kit that any customer could buy and that took advantage of the "head of household" Prohibition loophole. The kit provided yeast and paraphernalia to make wine at home. The company increased its sales force, added delivery trucks, and developed a sales campaign to move the juice throughout New York State and beyond.

Finger Lakes wineries that offered grape juice during Prohibition often referred to their products as wine-types. The Taylor brothers went a step farther; they not only capitalized the letters to give *Wine-Types* a prominent position on their labels, as if it were a special brand, but they also gave each individual juice the name of a well-known European wine. Taylor Wine-Types promised home winemakers that by following the step-by-step instructions that came with the juices they could produce Chablis, Burgundy, Rhine, and all manner of famous wines right in their basement. Throughout Prohibition, Taylor was the only Finger Lakes wine company either to maintain or to increase its grape tonnage purchases each year. Between 1919 and 1927, Taylor paid between $100 and $127 a ton for native grapes. Adjusted for inflation, those prices today would be above two thousand dollars per ton. Sadly, the actual prices for grapes today are stagnant and not much beyond the dollar amounts Taylor paid during Prohibition.

The eighteenth article of amendment to the Constitution of the United States is hereby repealed.

—Section One of the Twenty-First Amendment to the
U.S. Constitution, December 5, 1933

Fifteen simple words opened the floodgates.

Added to the loopholes in Prohibition legislation was one that allowed wineries that held inventory on the eve of the law's enactment to keep that inventory in storage during Prohibition (many in Congress did not believe that Prohibition would last as long as it had). Soon after Repeal, this inventory, which was estimated in the millions of gallons across the country, was unleashed on the market. Large Finger Lakes wineries were among the inventory holders, and they were quickly up and running: the Pleasant Valley Wine Company (doing business as Great Western), the Urbana Wine Company (doing business as Gold Seal), the Widmer Wine Company, and Taylor (renamed once again, this time to the Taylor Wine Company). Not only did Taylor have inventory to release, but the three Taylor brothers who had been operating the company through the Prohibition years after their father died had also been modernizing it with cash from its wildly successful juice business. When Repeal arrived, the company had the capacity to produce about half a million gallons of wine annually. The following year, Taylor added sparkling wine to its roster, joining Great Western and Gold Seal in boosting the Finger Lakes region to the title of sparkling wine capital of the country. When the Finger Lakes wine industry regained its momentum, the Taylor Wine Company emerged as the Northeast's indisputable leader.

Before the Taylor Wine Company's introduction of the tractor to Finger Lakes vineyards in 1948, much of grape growing in the region was still rather primitive; "primitive" also describes the wine grape varieties they continued to use. The year before Repeal, in his 1932 book *History of Central New York,* author Harry R. Melone identified twelve thousand grape acres cultivated by just over eleven hundred growers throughout the five Finger Lakes counties of Schuyler, Yates, Seneca, Steuben, and Ontario. Melone singled out three of the lakes—Keuka, Canandaigua, and Seneca—and he claimed that the Keuka Lake region "has proven itself the natural home to the grape, where it has developed to perfection." The grapes were field-hybrid "natives" like Catawba,

Isabella, and Concord. They were relatively easy to grow in the region, and Taylor continued to pay top dollar for them, a fact that attracted many Keuka dairy farm families.

Not only was operating a vineyard to supply Taylor profitable, but the timing of the work did not interfere with the cycle of dairy farming; as a bonus, animal manure was a good fertilizer for grapevines. Most dairy farmers got into grape growing strictly for the money. They had little, if any interest in upgrading, and so it was left up to the Taylor family to upgrade grape growing for them.

A misty morning on Canandaigua Lake, one of three lakes named by author Harry R. Melone as "the natural home to the grape." *Courtesy VisitFingerLakes.com.*

The dream of producing European-style wine in the United States had never died. California had been able to live the dream, but New York remained unable to do so. During Prohibition, and with abstainers at both legislative and private funding levels holding the purse strings, grape research done at the experiment station in Geneva was aimed mainly at table grape and juice production, with only a smattering of wine research. After Repeal, an effort to study grapes for making wine began to reshape at the agricultural station. In 1937, an article appeared in the *American Wine and Liquor Journal,* authored by Harry E. Gorseline of the US Department of Agriculture and Donald K. Tressler of the Geneva station, spelling out a program between the department and the station regarding overall fruit research, with special attention paid to winemaking research. By that time, the agricultural station had developed up to thirty thousand grape seedlings, the majority of which proved to have little or no commercial value. The station had also developed about twelve thousand promising hybrid seedlings, yet Finger Lakes winemakers were unfortunately recruited to help the scientists focus on and evaluate Concord grapes for wine, mainly because the variety did well in regional vineyards and because, mired in the past, scientists looked to pre-Prohibition wine consumption as a guide. Concord wine proved successful scientifically; it loved its Finger Lakes home and it produced proficiently. Commercially, however, Concord wine became a resounding failure.

Concord grapes, Naples, NY. Courtesy *VisitFingerLakes.com.*

In the Hudson Valley region, the grapes being introduced for wine a few years after Prohibition were the result of experiments done in Europe during the search for the cure to the *Phylloxera* blight. Referred to as French hybrids, these grape varieties were developed not as spontaneous field crosses like Catawba but in the laboratory, the way Reverend Bostwick at Keuka Lake had envisioned their development in 1833. The new hybrid varieties were classified as a species separate from the European as well as the many different North American species. Wines produced from French hybrids were supposed to be the middle ground, allowing New York to produce table wines with the subtlety of European wines from grapevines able to survive the northeastern environment, which European vines still could not do. The potential for success in the Finger Lakes with the French hybrids was an idea that had been recognized by Greyton H. Taylor, an executive at the winery that bore the family's name. The managing winemaker at Gold Seal Vineyards at the time also saw the potential for the hybrids.

In the tradition of hiring winemakers from the Champagne region of France, to restart the winery after Prohibition, Gold Seal brought Charles Fournier to the Finger Lakes from the Champagne city of Reims in 1934. This accomplished winemaker may or may not have known what to expect, but when he got to Gold Seal, his task was to produce wine from native grapes, and that included sparkling wine. Soon, Fournier was engaged with Philip Wagner in Maryland, the acknowledged "father" of French hybrid grape plantings in North America. Wagner was forever experimenting with the whole range of French hybrid varieties. Throughout the 1940s and '50s, Greyton Taylor and Fournier joined Wagner's experiments, sharing and arguing over the results.

By the 1950s, French hybrids were being blended with local grapes to "tone down" Finger Lakes wines. Some of the hybrids went into bottles as wines under their own names: Seyval Blanc, Aurore, Ravat, Chambourcin, Chancellor, Baco Noir, and more. Still, although they generally survived the northeastern climate as well as *Phylloxera*, the French hybrids would not live up to their promise as a replacement for European-style wines.

In 1950, other states were allowed in the California State Fair wine competition for the first time. Fournier sent Gold Seal Champagne, which to everyone's surprise won the only gold medal for sparkling wine. After the competition organizers discovered that the wine had been produced mainly from Catawba, wine produced outside California was never again allowed in the competition. Fournier was of course happy with the outcome, and the accolade catapulted Gold Seal to national prominence, but through his years as the company's chief winemaker Fournier itched to produce wine from the *Vitis vinifera* varieties that he knew from Europe. He got his shot that same year, after an encounter with a particularly interesting man at the agricultural station in Geneva.

Revolutionary Foundation

Konstantin Frank was an ethnic German who was born in the Soviet Union. He held a PhD in horticulture, with specific research on grapevines grown in cold climates. He had taught at the University of Odessa and later operated a winery in Ukraine. Being German and living in the USSR during the Second World War was problematic. Frank was forced to leave, but in Austria where he and his family wound up, they were seen as Soviets. The Frank family moved once more, to the United States.

Dr. Konstantin Frank
*Courtesy Dr. Konstantin Frank
Vinifera Wine Cellars*

His horticultural PhD, plus the fact that he spoke five languages but not English, landed Konstantin Frank a dishwashing job in New York City. There, he heard about the Finger Lakes wine region. Intent on regaining footing in grapevine research, Frank took his family to the Finger Lakes, where they settled in a small house. He applied for a position at the Geneva Agricultural Station, hoping to be allowed to research European vines in the region. He was convinced that he would get those vines to survive the region. Unfortunately, after much failure with European vine research, many at the agricultural station were wholly invested in working with native (with Concord at the top of the list) and French hybrid varieties. The best Frank could get from the American academics was a job at the station in Geneva as a laborer.

At a break in a meeting of the wine industry in Geneva, Konstantin Frank introduced himself to Charles Fournier by grabbing the Frenchman by the lapels. Speaking French, he made Fournier aware of his work with *vinifera* grapevines. The two overcame the fact that they were miles apart in temperament and focused on their mutual aspiration to produce Finger Lakes wine successfully from European grape varieties. Fournier was not just the Gold Seal winemaker; he was in charge of operations—in that capacity, he offered Frank the opportunity to proceed with his research under Gold Seal's auspices.

The collaboration of the two visionaries first paid off with a Riesling wine in 1956. Starting with that grape variety was a natural: Riesling's pedigree is German, produced in areas of that country that are similar to the Finger Lakes region's climate and topography. Fournier sent some of the wine to California for Gold Seal's then owner, Louis Benoist, to taste. Benoist liked the wine so much he had it all sent to him. Although that first Riesling was never commercially released, the reception it received proved to Fournier and Frank that they were on to something—they pressed on.

In 1962, with the release of Gold Seal Charles Fournier Riesling and Gold Seal Charles Fournier Chardonnay, the two men had fired the first shot in a Finger Lakes wine revolution.

Konstantin Frank soon developed his own grapevine nursery and winery at Keuka Lake, situated not far from Gold Seal. He proudly named his new business Dr. Konstantin Frank's Vinifera Wine Cellars. Like all revolutions, however, this one took time to build a following, and it had its detractors as well as its setbacks. During that time, French hybrid vineyard plantings and their wines grew in importance in the Finger Lakes region. Native and hybrid vineyards planted side by side had become common. The revolution didn't gain an effective army until the late 1970s.

6

A New Century for Dairy, Fruit, and Wine

OVER THE PAST FEW DECADES, New York's most important food products have faced and have overcome major hurdles to success. Premium Central New York cheese production gave way first to Wisconsin and then to the processed cheese industry; tasty Western New York apples were forced to compete with waxed, polished industrial-volume apples from the West Coast and from overseas; and the Finger Lakes wine industry was continually forced to live down a negative "native" wine reputation. In addition, high-volume products from Central and South America constantly threatened overall New York farm produce.

Modern Dairy Industry

The situation for local dairy farmers in the 1980s illustrated beautifully the farmer's sardonic complaint that his was the only business that bought at retail and sold at wholesale. Dairy farmers operated in an overall volatile market for raw material, the feed grain. The prices they paid to maintain their herds were not reflected in the prices that dealers paid for their milk. The situation kept dairy farmers in what can only be described as perpetual servitude. Around that time, many of the sons and daughters of struggling old-time dairy farmers returned to the farm with college degrees plus new ideas about food and its distribution. With self-reliance appealing to the prodigals, history was about to repeat itself in the Finger Lakes region: A small volume of milk could have its cream separated on the farm, butter production on the farm could be revived, and, more important, cheese could be made on a small scale and sold locally to augment the income from milk sales to dealers. If the idea worked, prices paid for cheese at retail would bring in more dollars per quart to the farmers than dealers were willing to pay for fresh milk. Many in the newly educated young crowd also wanted to reduce the environmental impact of large-scale farming on livestock, land, and local consumers.

Chèvre Spread
Courtesy of Lively Run Goat Dairy, Interlaken, New York

Ingredients

1 pound Lively Run Chèvre, plain

Local honey

Toasted almonds

Directions

Spread the chèvre in an oven safe dish. Cover with honey and top with almonds. Put in an oven on very low for 10 minutes, just to warm it up. Spread on crackers, bread, or shortbread cookies.

Courtesy Lively Run Goat Dairy.

The movement back to small Finger Lakes farm cheese production arguably began in 1982 when a sustainable farm started up in the small farming community of Interlaken situated between Seneca and Cayuga lakes. With its focus away from the bovine, Lively Run Goat Dairy was not the ordinary small dairy farm of the region's history, but with its primary market at first the always open-to-new-ideas college town of Ithaca, in Tompkins County, the goat cheese farm was an almost immediate success. For a time, Lively Run Goat Cheese was virtually the only small cheese success in the region, but only for a time. Soon enough, a few farmers began to produce small volumes of cheese from their Guernsey and Holstein herds.

By 2013, some Finger Lakes dairy farmer creameries were on the verge of using all their milk for cheese produced on the farm; before they got to that position, however, Central New York remained a major milk producer with a curtailed market. As it has always been, it took an immigrant to uncover a new opportunity. His name is Hamdi Ulukaya, and he is from Turkey.

Ulukaya came to New York in the late 1990s to study. After graduation, he stayed, leaving behind the possibility of becoming heir to his father's small cheese- and yogurt-manufacturing business in the old country that is supplied by the family dairy farm and from the milk of surrounding farms.

In 2005, Ulukaya had the opportunity to buy a defunct Kraft Foods cheese factory in New Berlin, New York, a Chenango County town settled in 1790 and situated in the area that had been the nineteenth-century center of cheese making in the United States. With the help of a loan, Ulukaya's vision of making better food available for more people became reality with the purchase of the facility. By 2007, his company, Chobani, was ready to launch a dairy product. Coming from a farming family, Ulukaya was well aware of the natureof his company's Central New York dairy farm surroundings (Chenango County Dairy Day is celebrated every summer at the fairgrounds as the county's number one industry). He named the company Chobani, because the word is taken from the Turkish word for "shepherd." Chobani would rely on the area's dairy farms to supply milk, and Ulukaya would shepherd his new product into the marketplace: Chobani Greek yogurt.

In the factory with Hamdi Ulukaya (right), founder and CEO of Chobani.
Courtesy of Chobani.

At first, Chobani received one daily truck of milk and had only five employees. By 2011, Chobani was established as the undisputed yogurt leader in a very old dairy category repurposed from a semi-liquid, heavily promoted "health" food to a thick, rich, still heavily promoted food. Unlike the claims of other yogurt producers, Chobani's health message was rendered valid because it is based on the product's lack of fillers and preservatives; the thick, creamy texture of the yogurt is an added bonus. In 2013, with more than two thousand employees, the Central New York factory was producing more than a million cases of Greek yogurt per week from an estimated twenty-four million pounds of milk supplied in stainless tanks by regional-area farms.

Despite its success, Chobani did not fully address the predicament in which twenty-first-century dairy farmers found themselves.

Bring Back Cheese

In 2010, excluding cottage cheese, total US cheese production was nearly 10.5 billion pounds, just over 3.5 percent more than in 2009—Wisconsin accounted for 25 percent of all cheese production. Even though it took more than a decade for the 1980s phenomenon of small cheese production to catch on in the Finger Lakes, when it did many participating dairy farmers found it surprisingly rewarding. In New York, the 2010 cheese production increased nearly 2 percent over 2009, to

Courtesy Finger Lakes Cheese Trail

almost 750 million pounds. A good deal of that cheese was produced from milk that farmers held back for their own cheese production. Reminiscent of Central New York's past, many Finger Lakes creameries today are small and family-operated. Some are run by the offspring of farming families with long-standing roots in the region; others by people who have turned to the farm as a life-changing alternative to the corporate or industrial world. Still, at first none of the dairy-farming families had resources for an advertising budget, not even to reach the local market.

In 2009, a number of local dairy farmers met to talk about ways to make their small farms more "visible" to the public. They knew that the region attracted thousands each year from within the intensely populated five-hundred-mile radius that encircles the Finger Lakes; they also knew that local wineries and wine trails were successfully tapping into that market. Dairy farmers wanted their group to become a "destination" for people to visit, to learn about their farming and cheese making, but—more important—to buy their handcrafted cheeses.

From the wineries, dairy families learned that something in the word *trail* appealed not only to the tourist but also to the locals, and so the

Finger Lakes Cheese Trail was born. Advertising in local periodicals like the *Finger Lakes Wine Gazette,* the group created its first "Finger Lakes Cheese Trail Open House" on Memorial Day weekend in 2010. The small creameries were unprepared for and overwhelmed by the turnout—and exceedingly gratified. The Open House became a standard annual event.

The Finger Lakes Cheese Trail proved that making cheese can again be a way of life for smaller farms, and while to some the primary motivation is to be independent from the milk plant, most of the trail's creameries continue to sell milk to a dealer, after they draw off enough milk to furnish their creamery—and some of that milk likely winds up as Chobani Greek yogurt.

With each passing year, local dairy farmers draw off more and more milk to meet a growing retail and wholesale demand for their handcrafted cheese. Rochester's Wegmans Food Markets has created a partnership with Cornell University's food science department to teach local dairy farmers how to make and age cheese. In 2013, Finger Lakes dairy farm cheeses were available in twelve local and regional grocers, eighty-five local wineries, and fifty New York restaurants.

Among the most exciting developments at the small dairy farms is a changeover to organic farming. The cows feed on organic food, and they are never pumped with antibiotics. Some of the farms produce non-pasteurized versions of their whole-milk cheeses as well. Not all the farms are certified organic, but just about all of them are stewards of land, animal, and food quality.

Muranda Cheese Company, part of the Finger Lakes Cheese Trail. *Courtesy Katherine Huysman Photography.*

Not all members of the cheese trail are open daily with a tasting and retail cheese shop to welcome the traveler. Unless you live nearby, you might not know the best time to stop by to pick up some cheese, because many of the farm families have a great deal of work on the farm to do and simply can't be in the retail shop all the time. Besides, many of the dairy farms are tucked away far from the main road. The public gets to meet the nearly dozen members of the Finger Lakes Cheese Trail throughout the year when they host their events. All events and information about the members are on the trail website: www. flcheesetrail.com.

Modern Apples

Finding it nearly impossible to compete with cheap produce and fruits imported into the country from South America and sold in large chain grocery stores, Finger Lakes farmers began to focus more stridently on the home market, giving rise in the 1980s to a proliferation of roadside stands and U-pick farms. All across the Finger Lakes, farmers sold fresh greens, tomatoes, and corn in season from small stands located right in front of the farms. Consumers could pay near-wholesale prices if they picked their own strawberries and cherries in spring, raspberries and stone fruits in summer, and pumpkins and apples in autumn; fresh-pressed apple cider has also appeared throughout the region, including that old colonial motivational liquid, the potent hard cider. That's because apples remain the most important fresh fruit crop of the region.

A U-pick farm in Naples, NY. *Courtesy VisitFingerLakes.com.*

Classic Apple Pie

Courtesy of nyapplecountry.com

Ingredients

Your favorite piecrust (homemade or store bought)—enough for a two-crust pie in a 9-inch pan

6 cups thinly sliced and peeled apples (Cortland, Empire, or Jonagold)

¼ cup sugar

2 tablespoons all-purpose flour

¾ teaspoon ground cinnamon

¼ teaspoon salt

⅛ teaspoon ground nutmeg

1 tablespoon lemon juice

Directions

1. Preheat the oven to 425°F.
2. Prepare the first piecrust (bottom), set it into the pan, press firmly, and then trim the crust edges even with the pan.
3. Combine all the remaining ingredients in a large bowl; mix lightly; fill the piecrust in the pan. Place the second piecrust over the top and wrap its excess under the bottom crust's edges.
4. Press the edges together to seal and flute.
5. With a knife, cut a few slits in the top crust.
6. Cover the edges with strips of aluminum foil and bake for 25 minutes; remove the foil and bake another 25 minutes or until golden brown.

Serves 8

When an agricultural marketing order for apples was established in 1959, creating a marketing fund for the promotion of New York State apples, it was an almost immediate success; apple growers have voted to renew it ever since. Over the years, from work in their experimental fruit orchards, Cornell's agricultural station scientists continued to introduce a number of hybrid apple varieties including but not limited to Spygold (1962), Empire (1966), Jonagold (1968), Jonamac (1972), Liberty (1978), and Fortune (1996). Apples were here to stay.

None of the apples with glistening waxed skin shipped into New York State and stacked at the produce section of large grocery chains provided the snap and crackle of fresh local apples that consumers could buy at the local apple store and produce market, where home-baked apple products and marmalades were also on display. The fall apple harvest created much local excitement, and since apples stored so very well, the annual crop stayed around as fresh as ever for months. The locals supported Finger Lakes apples precisely because of their freshness but also because the apple growers were neighbors.

After the dissolution of the New York and New England Apple Institute in 1994, when apple growers in the eastern part of the state joined the Western New York Apple Growers Association, they created the New York Apple Association. Together, the association's and the state Department of Agriculture's marketing order have increased the level of consumer knowledge of and interest in local apples. Under rules of the New York State Apple Marketing Order, the state Department of Agriculture assesses apple growers a fee on every bushel of apples they sell and then disburses that money to the apple association annually to cover programs to promote demand, advertise, oversee market research, and educate wholesale, retail, and consumer markets. The success of the marketing order was evident in the 1990s when the state averaged twenty-five million bushels of apples annually. Today, the growers' association includes almost seven hundred apple growers producing an average of thirty million bushels. That volume translates into ten thousand direct agricultural jobs and many thousands of indirect jobs in processing, packing, distributing, marketing, exporting, agricultural supplies, and ancillary apple industry services.

Perhaps no Finger Lakes-based fruit business better symbolizes the strength and depth of the apple's success than Red Jacket Orchards of Geneva, New York.

Red Jacket was the name of a Seneca who lived between 1750 and 1830. Even though the Seneca nation had sided with the British, Red Jacket negotiated the Treaty of Canandaigua with the United States after the Revolution (his name was taken from an embroidered red coat given to him by the British for his service). In the treaty, he managed to secure some land for those Seneca who did not retreat with the British to Canada; later, in the War of 1812, he sided with the United States.

Red Jacket was known for his oratory skills. His delivery of a speech in 1805 titled "Religion for the White Man and the Red" is preserved in Congress as one of the best examples of oratory in the new nation. His

birthplace is not known, but Red Jacket spent his youth near Branchport at the northeast branch of Keuka Lake, near Jemima Wilkinson's eighteenth-century religious settlement. He also lived a great deal of his life in the Genesee Valley region. Speculation concerning his birthplace includes one theory that he was born at Seneca Castle, outside Geneva, which is the reason that Fred Brownlee chose the name Red Jacket Orchards for his new orchard in Geneva in 1917.

Pruning trees at Red Jacket Orchards, located in Geneva NY along Seneca Lake. Courtesy Red Jacket Orchards

In 1958, Joe and Emily Nicholson were forced to close their poultry farm on Long Island to make way for yet another expressway to clog that region with cars. The Nicholsons went far enough away from Long Island—350 miles—to secure themselves against further expressways; they bought Brownlee's Red Jacket Orchards. From a small shed, they sold grapes, pears, raspberries, strawberries, and, their main crop, apples. Ten years later, the Nicholsons bought a rack and cloth fruit press to produce cider in their barn. By the 1990s, Red Jacket Orchards had grown its retail market, and it expanded into the wholesale farm market.

Red Jacket Orchards made its first trip to the New York City Greenmarket at Union Square in 1992; since then, it has become a weekly vendor in that venerable urban greenmarket where a variety of Finger Lakes produce is showcased. Red Jacket's expansion over the years has added to its thirty varieties of apples fruits like raspberries, cherries, blueberries, strawberries, plums, peaches, and apricots—it is the largest commercial apricot grower east of the Rocky Mountains. Joining its wholesale and retail fruit sales, Red Jacket added U-pick sales to consumers, plus it has developed a line of fruit juices with apples at its core.

Increasing its orchards meant that the company needed to keep the fruit as a consistent expression of its land and surrounding climate, which in turn meant looking into sustainable and organic fruit-growing and juice production methods. In 2006, Red Jacket Orchards installed nearly two acres of tunnels that provide a special growing environment for tender tree fruit crops like apricots. In 2009, it built a certified sustainable juice facility and distribution center, and in 2012 the company reinvigorated its organic initiatives by transitioning another portion of its fruit orchards to organic as well as biodynamic farming. That same year, Red Jacket installed bee boxes around its orchards to attract native bee populations and to augment the activities of traditional honeybees that local beekeepers supply to the orchards.

Of all its innovations and developments, Red Jacket's owners credit its connection to New York City's Greenmarkets for much of its success. Not only has this innovative farmers' market program put Red Jacket Orchards into the minds of urban shoppers, but—like the Erie Canal and the railroad of old—it also helps Finger Lakes produce vendors bring high-quality fruit to the attention of a massive population of consumers.

In 2013, out of thirty-six apple-producing states, New York was at the top in the number of commercial apple varieties produced (almost two dozen). The top ten apples sold were: McIntosh, Empire, Red Delicious, Cortland, Golden Delicious, Rome, Idared, Crispin, Paula Red, and—tied for tenth place—Gala, Jonagold, and Jonamac. More than half of the apples produced were sold as fresh fruit; the rest went to processing (almost five million bushels to juice and cider). The Finger Lakes region and Western and Central New York account for three out of the six apple-producing areas in the second largest apple-producing state in the United States.

Despite what appeared to be overwhelming competition from the West Coast and as far away as from New Zealand, the Finger Lakes apple industry has proved that it is here to stay, just like the other fruit, the one that led the Finger Lakes region's bounty into the twenty-first century: the grape.

Modern Wine Revolution

In the early 1970s, California was home to a number of small quality-oriented wine producers that emulated the best that Europe had to offer. Still, cheap bulk products dominated West Coast wine. Then, in 1976, in Paris, a major wine-tasting competition took place. It pitted famous Bordeaux and Burgundy wines against a few upstart California producers of Cabernet Sauvignon and Chardonnay, the two French grape varieties grown respectively in the two French regions in the competition. The event illustrated the true potential of small California producers when French wine professionals selected in a blind tasting some of the California wines over some of the most famous wines of France. Soon, US consumers began seeking premium California table wine at home. With this new interest came growth in wine consumption across the country, led mainly by the baby-boomer generation, which had grown up and established its own version of the middle class.

Tracking the baby-boomer generation, large corporations had been entering the wine business since the late 1960s. Riding on the crest of the increased consumption of the 1970s, corporate giants of the food and spirits industries feverishly raced to buy up venerable wine companies. Corporations gobbled California wine companies where most of the country's giant wineries were situated—Almaden, Paul Masson, Inglenook, Italian Swiss Colony, and more. New York was the only other state with a few giant wine companies, and they were situated in the Finger Lakes. The conglomerates went for them, too: Seagram bought Gold Seal, French's Foods bought Widmer, and Coca-Cola bought Taylor Great Western (Taylor had taken over Great Western in the early 1960s).

Still operating in the small village of Hammondsport, where the Finger Lakes wine industry began in the 1850s, Taylor Great Western ranked sixth nationally in wine production; it had made the village of Hammondsport into a "company town," and it was supporting thousands of employees, grape growers, and other vendors when Coca-Cola bought the company in 1977. Coke's entry into the Keuka wine business caused a major rift in the community between those on the side of local grape growers and the corporate people with no allegiance to the region. Leading the animosity toward Coke was the grandson and namesake of Taylor's founder, Walter Taylor.

Once an executive at Great Western, Walter Taylor began to speak out against corporate winery ownership of his once family-owned business. He aimed specific vitriol at the practice of using California wine to blend with (and "tone down") Keuka wine. As the dominant regional wine producer, Taylor was canceling what had been long-standing, lucrative contracts with hundreds of Finger Lakes grape growers, which Walter also railed against. To get his message to the consumer, Walter used the new winery that he had built on part of the Taylor family's original homestead on the Bully Hill, and that he named Bully Hill Vineyards. His wine labels got across to the public that his was the only winery that could rightfully apply the Taylor name to its labels; it was a message that started a major legal battle between Walter Taylor and Coca-Cola. The fight centered on Walter's claim that his was the original Taylor company that his grandfather passed down from that very spot on Bully Hill where it had been conceived.

The court noted that the deed to the original property remained at the

Walter Taylor and his goat "Guilt-Free." Taylor often posed for photos with this goat, supporting his declaration that "They took my name, but they did not get my goat." Courtesy Taylor Wine Museum.

RIGHT: Courtesy VisitFingerLakes.com.

Taylor Wine Company, now owned by Coke, and that Taylor could be used on Bully Hill Vineyards labels only to identify the winery's owner—never to promote the brand name. Not happy with these restrictions, Walter saw the promotional value in claiming that the court had taken away his name. Instead of relabeling his wines as he was instructed to do, he drew a thick black line through his name on the labels; he also created a slogan, "They took my name, but they did not get my goat," and added a drawing of a goat. The media confused the issue, which gave Walter an opportunity to gain national recognition. Coverage of Walter's additional antics, which were many, eventually catapulted Bully Hill Vineyards from a small family operation into the national big leagues, creating an annual flow of tourists to the Finger Lakes just to visit the maverick's business.

While the big companies fought it out in the marketplace, small wineries in California were poised to take center stage after their success at the 1976 tasting in Paris. The same thing was about to happen in New York. The coverage of Walter Taylor's court case brought general attention to a revitalized Finger Lakes wine industry that consisted of small wineries, just as it had when the local wine industry started in the mid-nineteenth century. This time the new crop of wineries was not confined to Keuka Lake; they also operated at Canandaigua, Seneca, and Cayuga lakes. In the late 1970s and early '80s, joining Konstantin Frank's already venerable Vinifera Wine Cellars came wineries with names like Heron Hill Vineyards, Chateau Esperanza, Finger Lakes Wine Cellars, McGregor Vineyards, Casa Larga Vineyards, Glenora Wine Cellars, Hermann J. Wiemer Vineyards, Wagner Vineyards, Plane Vineyards, and Knapp Vineyards.

Walter Taylor and the court case notwithstanding, the newly developing Finger Lakes wine industry would have been unable to gain traction had it not been for the New York State legislature's Farm Winery Act of 1976, enacted the same year as the Paris tasting that helped the California wine industry. Until the Farm Winery Act, the price for a New York permit to start a winery was uniform and expensive, no matter the size of the winery. A New York winery was also not allowed to have a wine-tasting room that was open to the public, and to get its wine into retail shops, a winery had to sell at wholesale through an alcohol distributor. The farm winery legislation reduced the price of a permit to a few hundred dollars for wineries under a certain annual production volume, opened winery tasting rooms to consumers, and allowed small wineries to sell direct to retailers. Later changes in the legislation increased the allowable annual production, provided a way for wineries to open up to five satellite tasting locations within the state, and either dismantled or adjusted a number of other regulations that continued to put undue burdens on small wineries.

The plan of some small Finger Lakes winery owners who had been grape growers for years was to establish a new market for their crops. Many had large plantings of French hybrid and native grape varieties to market, but that market for their grapes was drying up as larger regional wineries systematically lost market share for their generic bulk wines.

For many grape growers the solution was to learn how to produce better table wine from these grapes and to sell the wines directly to the public. Many of the newly established small wineries also planned to build on Konstantin Frank's success with European grape varieties. It would take at least four years for their *vinifera* plantings to start producing viable crops, and because it was still risky, *vinifera* plantings were not yet extensive.

By 1980, however, small as it was, the few Finger Lakes *vinifera* wines produced in the latter part of the previous decade had gained the attention of the press, including the *New York Times*. The well-respected *Times* wine writer Frank Prial began to give more coverage to the region than the newspaper had given before (a new wine writer at the newspaper, Howard Goldberg, soon came on the scene to give special emphasis to the developments in New York wine). Momentum raised expectations that in the 1980s more Finger Lakes varietal wines with names like Riesling, Chardonnay, and Pinot Noir on their labels would show up in the marketplace. Unfortunately, on Christmas Day 1980, the temperature dropped across the Finger Lakes region from a high of thirty-five degrees Fahrenheit to as low as fifteen below zero in some locations. Known as "the Christmas Massacre," the result was widespread devastation in regional vineyards, affecting all grapevine species, but especially the tender *vinifera*.

Those who followed Konstantin Frank's advice to "hill up" the vineyard rows after harvest to protect root systems by burying them in extra layers of soil lost in the massacre the buds for the coming vintage but not the vines. Those who disregarded his advice lost the vines. It took a few years for damaged vines that did survive to revitalize; it took even more years to replant the vines that did not, delaying the *vinifera* revolution. The revolution would have been delayed even further were it not for three things: the dogged insistence of Konstantin Frank in developing grapevine stock clones that would survive the disease-inducing humidity of the region as well as the erratic winters; the survival performance of Gold Seal's *vinifera* vineyards that Charles Fournier had planted years earlier, in what he determined were the warmer sections around Seneca Lake, an area that today growers refer to as "the banana belt"; and the observations of winemaker Hermann Wiemer.

A German immigrant who had been taught at Germany's best wine production college, and who came to the United States to make wine at Bully Hill Vineyards, Hermann Wiemer was in the market in 1980

Hermann J.
Wiemer, founder
of Wiemer
Vineyards.
*Courtesy Megan
Dailor*

for a suitable site to establish his own winery. Along State Route 14, which runs north–south on the west side of Seneca Lake, he carefully observed plant life in and around a site that appealed to him. He concluded that the site had been reasonably protected from the Christmas massacre; that's where he decided to establish a winery based solely on *Vitis vinifera* grapevines, which he assumed—correctly—would also be protected at the site. Until the mid-1990s, Konstantin Frank's winery at Keuka Lake and Hermann Wiemer's winery at Seneca Lake were the only ones in the region solely concentrated on *vinifera* wines, and they were the only Finger Lakes wineries to gain international recognition.

Still, small wineries continued to appear along the lakes' shores with pleasing regularity during the mid- and late 1980s, as the market for native wines slipped precipitously. For long-standing regional grape-growing families invested in the native varieties, the decade was a major disaster. Newspaper accounts of vineyards being bulldozed and farm equipment auctioned off were common. The large wineries under conglomerate control, which had reduced their grape purchases, began to close. The last and most successful of them, Taylor Great Western, died in 1995, after a collective 135 years in operation at Keuka Lake. The small wineries of the region were on their own; most had neither funds nor marketing savvy to grow much beyond their tasting room sales.

In 1985, the New York legislature stepped in once again, this time with the establishment of the New York Wine and Grape Foundation. The state provided funding and a mandate to promote the grape and wine industries as well as to fund grape and wine research. The organization made it possible for small wineries to pool their resources, not just to market their wines but also to develop the state's wine regions as tourist destinations. The Finger Lakes was the largest wine region in the state, and the first region to understand and capitalize on this new money by creating a model of winery cooperative marketing known as the "wine trail."

The cooperative wine trail phenomenon started at Cayuga Lake and then quickly spread to Keuka and Seneca lakes. The trail idea, plus other promotional venues like the annual Finger Lakes Wine Festival—begun at Cayuga Lake in the early 1990s and later moved to the Watkins Glen Racetrack—as well as a series of events sponsored by the Wine and Grape Foundation throughout the state, raised awareness and helped increase the number of Finger Lakes wineries from a few dozen in the 1980s to about a hundred at the start of the twenty-first century. While the region's wineries still offered products from three species of grapevines—North American, French hybrid, and European—the focus turned to the latter.

Konstantin Frank's Vinifera Wine Cellars at Keuka Lake, is half a century old and in its third generation of family ownership. The winery has gained international recognition for its grapevine nursery, its wines, and its role as the leading wine producer that helped put Finger Lakes wine on the world stage. The key to Frank's initial work was to develop and duplicate particular grapevine selections through painstaking trial-and-error breeding so that the resulting vines were designed for the region and its erratic weather. Riesling was the one grapevine that Konstantin Frank was certain would be right at home in the region. Its natural home being the mountain regions of Germany, as a cool-climate wine grape Riesling proved Frank correct in its ability to survive and for its resulting wines to excel. Soon, the rest of the wine world

discovered what is the Finger Lakes region's singularly spectacular wine achievement. The international wine community now gives Finger Lakes Riesling its due in magazine articles in print and online, as well as a continuing string of achievement awards for Rieslings in wine competitions at home and abroad. Today, no matter what its focus, nearly every Finger Lakes winery offers at least one version of Riesling wine.

Along with Riesling, a number of Finger Lakes winemakers have begun to renew the region's past sparkling wine supremacy, this time not from Catawba grapes but from Pinot noir and Chardonnay, the classic wine grapes of France's cool-climate Champagne region that, again thanks to Konstantin Frank, have proven themselves locally.

It's always been understood that, for technical reasons that have to do with grape maturity, white wine grapes are more suitable than red wine grapes in cool climates. Slowly, however, Finger Lakes wine producers have been changing that view with grape varieties like Cabernet franc, a grape that grows well in France's west and northwest regions, and the Lemberger grape (known as Blaufrankisch in its Austrian home). In each case, the red grapes have already proven themselves in cooler climates abroad; now they are proving themselves in the Finger Lakes region.

Riesling Wine Jelly
Courtesy of the author

Equipment
Water bath canner with directions

Five 8-ounce jelly jars with lids and rings

Ingredients
1 750ml bottle dry Finger Lakes Riesling wine

1 package powdered pectin (3 ½ tablespoons)

4 cups sugar

Directions
1. Follow directions to sanitize the jars and lids.
2. Bring the wine to a simmer in a pot; remove the pot from the heat and let sit, covered, for 25 to 30 minutes or until cooled.
3. Mix the pectin in well, breaking up any lumps.
4. Bring the mixture to a boil; stir constantly until the boil threatens to foam over the pot. Then add the sugar while still stirring until it comes to a second full boil. Boil for at least 1 minute, then turn off heat. Also, bring water in the canner to a boil.
5. Quickly skim any foam off the top of the jelly, and give it one last stir to create bubbles; then fill each of the five hot, sanitized jars.
6. Seal the jars and follow the directions to process in your water bath canner.

Through a series of rotating wine- and food-centric events, the New York Wine and Grape Foundation is behind much of the message concerning Finger Lakes wine that goes out to the world. The rest of the fervor and interest is generated at the wineries themselves, through tasting room consumer contact as well as at special events. At each of the wine producing Finger Lakes, wineries pool their resources with a selection of cooperative special events throughout the year, concentrating mainly on seasons and holidays, with added events that they take to restaurants and wine shops, farmers' and crafts markets, local fairs, and the New York State Fair, as well as fund-raising events and even political gatherings. More important than cooperative marketing, Finger Lakes winemakers are in constant dialogue among themselves: They dine together regularly, they learn together at short courses sponsored by the Geneva Agricultural Experiment Station, and some winemakers at a few separate wineries have joined together to produce special collaborative wines.

Since the beginning of the modern wine revolution, wine writers and critics have consistently named the Finger Lakes an "emerging wine region." These days, on almost any given day of the year, Finger Lakes wine representatives can be found throughout New York State and beyond, taking the following message to market: After 150 years, the Finger Lakes wine industry has gone beyond "emerging." It has arrived.

7

The Past as Future

THE OVERALL CENTRAL NEW YORK region has a bright and continuing future before it, but it's clear that this future would not be possible without the efforts of many in the past. Take as an example Enos Boughton and his three sons, the first settlers to farm what is today the intersection in Victor, New York, at Boughton Hill Road and State Route 444, in the northwest corner of Ontario County. This was an Iroquois site, which was abandoned in 1687 after a French attack on the Seneca nation.

In 1935, A. C. Parker of the Rochester Museum, the same man who began excavation of the Lamoka site between Keuka and Seneca lakes, oversaw J. Sheldon Fisher's archaeological survey of the Boughton Hill area. In 1959 Fisher, now the Ontario County historian, submitted plans to the National Park Service for the preservation of the site. In 1963, the National Park Service's John Cotter noted on the application form: "A site well deserving preservation, and should receive no less than National Landmark status . . ."

Boughton Hill was entered on the National Register of Historic Places in 1966 as the site of the significant seventeenth-century Seneca village, Gannagaro. The following year, the Gannagaro Association was formed to promote the site's preservation; the association received a $350,000 grant in 1970 from the state's Executive Budget. More grants followed and more site preservation ensued until, on July 14, 1987, the Ganondagan State Historical Site was formally dedicated. Two years later, the Friends of Ganondagan, Inc., was formed as a not-for-profit educational organization to support the Ganondagan State Historic Site.

Photo courtesy VisitFingerLakes.com.

In 1992, plans for a longhouse construction on the site began. The longhouse was completed by 1998, in time for a state visit by then First Lady Hillary Rodham Clinton, during the White House Millennium Council tour that summer. In 2004, plans for an Art & Education Center on the site began, and in 2007, the First Annual Native Food Fest was held there; it was also the beginning of interest in what became the collaborative Iroquois White Corn Project between the Brooklyn, New York–based Heritage Foods USA and the Friends of Ganondagan. The project revived a two-thousand-year-old staple of the Iroquois diet.

According to Heritage Foods USA, "All Iroquois White Corn Products originate from corn seeds that descended from seeds planted in the 1600s. The seed has been carefully managed and protected by Haudenosaunee (Iroquois) farmers for 2,000 years to keep the genetics pure. Iroquois White Corn has not been genetically modified. The Iroquois White Corn is hand harvested, dried, and roasted. Each bag is ground to order to retain its natural freshness."

Heritage Foods USA packages three varieties of white corn—aromatic, nutty hulled corn; roasted corn flour; and an earthy-tasting regular corn flour. A portion of the proceeds of the sale of the white corn products goes to the nonprofit Friends of Ganondagan to support the Ganondagan State Historic Site.

Back to the Roots

The white corn project fits nicely into a food movement that has spread across the United States. Younger generations understand that the first step to taking care of body and soul is to take care of the land—and to know your food source. The movement has been coined "locavore."

Locavore is a nod to the past, when working the land meant knowing where your food came from and knowing that it was wholesome, in a time when farming was local. Many consumers today want to know not only who raised the livestock and cultivated the crops, but also how and why they did it. They want their food minimally processed, without the use of petrochemicals or, in the case of livestock, antibiotics. They want their food fresh, and they want it close to home.

Overall, Finger Lakes regional farmers have embraced the local food movement, from the farmer at Lakeview Organic Grain in Penn Yan who

Three Sisters Vegetable Soup

Courtesy of the Iroquois White Corn Project at Ganondagan in Victor, New York

Prepare the corn ahead so that it will be ready to add to soups, stews, chili, and salads.

Soak 1 cup of Heritage Foods USA Hulled White Corn in water overnight
(yields 2 to 3 cups cooked corn).

Drain and rinse the corn, place it in a stockpot, add water to cover by 3 inches, and bring to a boil.

Reduce the heat to low and cook for 4 to 5 hours, depending on your texture preference (4 hours for a firmer texture, until a few kernels pop; 5 hours for a softer texture with the majority of the kernels popped).

If you want to use fresh dried beans, soak 1 pound of dried kidney or pinto beans overnight in a pot of water; drain the next day, refill the pot with water, and slow-cook until the beans are tender.

Alternative Crock-Pot Preparation: Place the dried corn in a Crock-Pot. Add water to cover by 3 inches. Cook 6 ½ hours on high setting or 10 hours on low. Drain and rinse.

Ingredients for Soup

2 tablespoons olive oil	2 cups peeled and cubed winter squash
1 cup chopped onions	1 cup diced carrots
2 celery stalks (chopped)	1 cup cubed parsnips
2 cloves minced garlic	Two 15 ½-ounce cans diced tomatoes (or diced fresh tomatoes)
1 teaspoon dried basil	2 cups cooked Heritage Foods USA Hulled White Corn
1 teaspoon cumin	1 pound kidney or pinto beans (if canned, drain and rinse)
Salt and pepper to taste	Vegetable stock or water

Directions

1. Warm the oil in a large soup pot on medium heat.
2. Add the onions, celery, and garlic; sauté about 10 minutes on low.
3. Add the basil, cumin, and salt and pepper to taste.
4. Add the squash, carrots, parsnips, and tomatoes; cover and simmer until tender.
5. Add the corn and beans; simmer for another 10 minutes.
6. Add enough vegetable stock or water to make the soup as liquid as you want.

Serves about 8

grows a number of heirloom wheat varieties to farmers across the region who, along with the staple onion, potato, tomato, asparagus, corn, and many fruit crops, have taken an interest in reviving crops of the past: cabbage, beans, squash, all kinds of berries, a multitude of herbs, and even the seemingly esoteric like the rhizomes rhubarb and wild fiddleheads that have historically fostered a kind of open secret society in the region. Joining the movement is a large contingent of Amish and Mennonite families that have been moving into the Finger Lakes region over the past couple of decades, two cultures that have historically favored local over industrial farming.

Local consumers now have access to fresh Finger Lakes produce and meats as well as quality packaged items produced and processed in the region, from squash and grape seed oils to berry jams and fruit pies to fresh nitrite-free bacon from hogs that roam and forage the Finger Lakes terrain. Also available are local poultry, lamb, and beef as well as exotic meats like ostrich and bison.

Wild Edible Ferns

North America is home to three species of wild edible ferns: ostrich *(Matteucia struthiopteris)*, lady *(Athyrium filix-femina)*, and bracken *(Pteridium aquilinum)*. The edible part of each is the young, tender shoot, a curled tip that resembles the top of a fiddle—the fiddlehead. The shoots emerge in spring and early summer. Once they mature, the fern fronds should never be eaten—*ever*—unless you like extreme bitterness.

The ostrich is the most commonly known fiddlehead fern in these parts. This is the species often available in produce markets. It grows in shady river bottoms, and occasionally in rich hardwood forests. Ostrich ferns are abundant in the Great Lakes, the Northeast, and much of southern Canada.

Fiddlehead stalks are smooth, and the coiled tops are full of brown flakes. A deep trough runs the length of the top of the stalk in a U-shape. Fiddleheads are too old to gather by the time leaves are fully formed on sugar maples and oaks. Harvested before the leafy portion of the frond is open, the fiddleheads snap right off with a twist.

Ramps

Fern shoots should not be eaten raw. Boiled or steamed and served with butter like asparagus, fiddleheads are tasty. With another local spring delight, ramps (sometimes in season at the same time as fiddleheads), the dish is delicious.

Fiddleheads: An Old and Simple Recipe

1. Wash fiddleheads thoroughly; boil them for 5 minutes and drain.
2. Slice off the ends of ramps, chop them finely, and sauté in butter; add the fiddleheads and sauté until all is tender.

The cornerstone of the locavore movement is sustainability, a concept that may but doesn't necessarily mandate either organic or biodynamic methods (each a so-called natural method of farming that must be certified). Because of the overall view that farmers are stewards of the land, whether for orchard, field crops, or livestock, the farms that

LEFT: A vegetable table at a Finger Lakes area farmer's market. *Courtesy VisitFingerLakes.com.*

do not gain organic or biodynamic certification still practice as many sustainable farming methods as they can.

Nowhere in the Finger Lakes is the locavore movement better illustrated than at the Ithaca Farmers Market. The market began in the 1970s and has been growing ever since. This expansion has caused it to change location five times. A few years ago, needing more space and seeking to act on its philosophy of sustainability, the Ithaca Farmers Market reclaimed and upgraded an abandoned steamboat landing in the city. Now situated along the refurbished dock with a pavilion at its far end, the market is open every Saturday and Sunday. Its members also participate in two smaller markets: in downtown Ithaca on Tuesdays, and at a nearby shopping mall on Wednesdays.

The Ithaca Farmers Market at the base of Cayuga Lake.

In 2007 and 2008, the market initiated waste management composting and consumer packaging concepts to reduce its impact on the environment.

With more than 160 members in 2013, the Ithaca Farmers Market was the largest in the region. It allows only vendors who live within thirty miles of the city and boasts that consumers will find neither bananas nor pineapples in this locally focused food market. Every plant food available at the Ithaca Farmers Market is seasonal; the market publishes a crop calendar that traces the growing season and the extent to which a particular crop is available for consumption. It covers so many foods that the market is open for part of the winter, too, to provide a market outlet for the growing number of greenhouse farmers.

In addition to farmers' markets, where local greens, fruits, meats, eggs, cheeses, and baked goods are sold, U-pick farms have continued to proliferate in the region. Many of these farms are owned and worked by the influx of Mennonite and Amish families that have over the past twenty years contributed to the local economy their own brand of self-sufficiency. For livestock, small family farms in the region raise poultry, hogs, lamb, ostrich, bison, and beef steers on open ranges. The meats are sent to slaughter under US Department of Agriculture supervision and then sold on the farm and at farmers' markets or cooperatives. The eggs from poultry farms present deep orange yolks and rich flavors.

The region is home to a number of food cooperatives. Once again, Ithaca is in the vanguard. For a small annual fee—nine dollars in 2013—GreenStar Cooperative members shop at two large grocery stores that primarily offer organically produced foods, with local producers given first priority on the shelves and in the coolers and freezers. GreenStar members enjoy a discount on every purchase.

Another Finger Lakes regional cooperative that began in 2000 has education and collaboration as its goals. Its mission statement says it all: "Finger Lakes Culinary Bounty (FLCB) is a collaborative regional food network that helps educate consumers about locally-produced foods and beverages while fostering relationships within the marketplace."

FLCB stems from a culinary tourism conference sponsored by Cornell Cooperative Extension and the Cayuga County Office of Tourism;

Courtesy Finger Lakes Culinary Bounty.

it was held in Auburn, New York, in 1999. The keynote speaker, Henri Benveniste—then chef at the Aurora Inn at the north end of Cayuga Lake—spoke rapturously of the French concept of *terroir*, where soil and climate combine to create local uniqueness. He spoke of how he applied the *terroir* concept in his locally infused menu at the inn. Chef Henri issued a challenge to the attendees, representatives from Finger Lakes food and wine industries: to collectively promote the region's bounty by including local foods and wines in the menus at restaurants; to demand local foods and wines in regional grocers and wine shops; for food purveyors to collaborate with one another; and for the food and wine industries to lobby legislators for regulations to make it simpler and less costly to provide local abundance.

After this rousing challenge, a group met monthly to develop a regional food network for the Finger Lakes. From those early meetings came the Finger Lakes Culinary Bounty, aimed at highlighting the region's food and wine production, with a focus on networking. More than 150 members throughout the fourteen Finger Lakes counties have been representing the local food, beverage, and tourism industries for just over a decade. In this capacity, Finger Lakes Culinary Bounty has built a regional network that connects food and drink producers with end users—restaurants, grocers, farmers' markets, and consumers. The organization also stays on top of government intervention in licensing and regulations.

Local Wine and Culinary Corporate Sponsorship

From its headquarters in Fairport, New York, Constellation Brands fluctuates today between being the second and third largest wine company in the world. The corporation got its humble start after the Second World War when the Sands family bought a manufacturing building in Canandaigua to form the Canandaigua Wine Company. Between the 1940s and 1980s, the family-operated firm was the smaller brother to the giant wine companies of the region, Taylor Great Western, Gold Seal, and Widmer. Realizing in the 1980s that for existing Finger Lakes wineries it was either grow or go, the Sands family decided to act. Their idea was to add to their already successful line of low-end domestic wine products with recognized names and international markets. While corporate conglomerates were failing with their acquisitions of domestic wineries, the tiny, local Canandaigua Wine Company first began to acquire international brands and then made domestic acquisitions—which in the end included the very Finger Lakes wineries that once overshadowed it in the home market.

The Canandaigua Wine Company is today just a part of the overall giant Constellation Brands and, while family control remains, the company is global and on the public stock market. Its connection to the Finger Lakes region remains in the company's small annual purchase of local grape crops and in its sponsorship of the New York Wine and Culinary Center.

The mission of the New York Wine and Culinary Center "is to educate, engage and excite visitors by celebrating and showcasing New York's finest wine, food and agriculture . . . in a setting that proudly highlights the natural beauty, rich history and agricultural bounty of New York State . . ."

To that end, since its opening in 2006, the Wine and Culinary Center in Canandaigua has offered cooking classes focused on local ingredients, a wine program that leads to a Master Sommelier certificate, a bistro, banquet catering, and a New York beverage-tasting room.

Wines from the Canandaigua Wine Trail. *Courtesy VisitFingerLakes.com.*

Apple-Pear Bread Pudding with Cinnamon Maple Sauce

Courtesy of Michael Sokolski, executive chef at the New York Wine and Culinary Center

Bread pudding originated in England in the thirteenth century. Early settlers brought this dessert to North America, but it was called hasty pudding, and it was made with cornmeal instead of wheat.

Ingredients

1 tablespoon soft butter

Fruit

3 tablespoons butter
3 New York Emerald apples
3 New York Bartlett pears
¼ cup brown sugar
Pinch of ground cinnamon

Custard

7 eggs
2 cups milk
2 cups heavy cream
¾ cup white sugar
½ teaspoon ground cinnamon
Pinch of ground nutmeg
1 teaspoon vanilla extract

Bread

4 cups cubed bread
¼ cup melted butter
¼ cup white sugar
Pinch of ground cinnamon

Custard Add-Ins

1 cup walnuts
1 cup raisins

Cinnamon-Maple Sauce

2 cups heavy cream
¼ cup maple syrup
Pinch of ground cinnamon

Directions

1. Preheat the oven to 350°F. Grease a 13 x 9-inch baking pan with the tablespoon of soft butter.

Fruit

2. Peel, core, and cut the apples and pears into "dice-sized" cubes.

1. Melt the butter in a saucepan. Add the cubed fruit and cook for a few minutes over medium heat, until the fruit starts to soften.

2. Add the brown sugar and cinnamon. Cook for another couple of minutes, until the brown sugar dissolves. Take the pan off the heat and set it aside to cool.

Bread

3. Spread the bread cubes on a baking tray and drizzle with the melted butter. Sprinkle the sugar and cinnamon on top.

4. Toss everything together, distributing the ingredients evenly.

5. Bake in the preheated oven for about 10 minutes, until lightly brown. Cool and set aside. Maintain the oven temperature.

Custard

6. Whisk the eggs together in a bowl.

7. Add the milk, cream, sugar, cinnamon, nutmeg, and vanilla. Whisk together well. Set aside.

Assemble Bread Pudding

8. Place the toasted bread in the buttered 13 x 9-inch pan.

9. Whisk the custard and pour it over the bread. Distribute the cooked apples and pears, with any juice, evenly throughout the pan. Sprinkle half of the walnuts and all of the raisins evenly over the mixture. With a spoon, press down any ingredients that may be sticking up. Sprinkle the remaining walnuts over the top.

10. Place the pan in 350°F oven and bake for about 40 to 50 minutes, or until the center puffs up.

Cool and serve with sauce and or whipped cream.

Sauce

11. Place the cream, maple, and cinnamon in a bowl. Whisk the mixture until it thickens but is still soft.

Makes one 13 x 9-inch pan; serves 12–15

In 2013, the *Huffington Post* named the Finger Lakes number three in its top ten world wine regions to visit and suggested that the New York Wine and Culinary Center is the place to start a tour of the region, for its regional food and for its wine education. All very true—but the culinary center is not alone in the region for showcasing locally produced foods. Many Finger Lakes restaurants proudly announce on their menu that the food is sourced locally. Together with the many regional organizations and cooperatives, these restaurants host a series of special wine and food events throughout the year, with an emphasis on seasonal menus. Growers and producers send representatives to these special wine tastings and dinners.

Media and Events

Local media is involved in the locavore movement as well, and no one better represents that development than the city of Rochester's Michael Warren Thomas, whose radio program and website, *Savor Life,* has focused on and promoted Finger Lakes food and drink since the 1990s. Thomas interviews local farmers, winemakers, chefs, and food and wine writers on his show, and he sponsors a variety of events and dinners around the region. In 2013, Thomas developed a motivational listing program to persuade Finger Lakes restaurants to offer wine lists with a minimum 30 percent locally produced wines. His idea had area restaurants actively vying for a position at the top of his list, which he periodically updates for listeners and readers.

Responsible for at least one major ingredient in the Finger Lakes region's bounty, the New York Wine and Grape Foundation has successfully developed numerous venues throughout any given year to promote not only regional wine but also regional foods, especially wine's good companion, cheese. The foundation presents wines and cheeses to major cities in the United States and abroad, and has enlisted politicians both in the New York State capitol as well as members of the New York contingent in both the House and Senate in Washington—where, along with the New York Farm Bureau, the foundation has developed an annual New York Farm Days presentation.

In a series of events throughout the year, the Finger Lakes Culinary Bounty organization brings consumers closer to the source of their food and drink. At the head of the list of events is the annual Finger Lakes Restaurant Week, a celebration of local restaurateurs, farmers, and food and drink organizations supporting the local food movement. Each autumn, about a dozen restaurants scattered throughout the Finger Lakes region offer special meals at special prices to highlight an array of fresh, locally produced food and drink during an entire week. The organization also sponsors an annual Finger Lakes Cork and Fork event, to showcase packaged non-perishables produced from local ingredients by small, often family-run local companies.

Each year at fall harvesttime, Finger Lakes Culinary Bounty organizes its Harvest Dinner to highlight the many fruits, nuts, and vegetables that come rolling in. The event calls on local chefs to collaborate in the

Conehead cabbage at a farmer's market.
Courtesy Sherry Burford.

kitchen, producing an exciting blend of food concepts and presentation. The dinner includes the products of selected farmers, drinks producers, and product manufacturers, who turn locally harvested produce into items for the pantry. The event is often hosted by regional luminaries in the food and drink community like Michael Warren Thomas of *Savor Life* Radio.

Finally, New York State produces the second largest quantity of wine in the United States after California. In 2013, of the 320 New York wineries in twelve regions of the state—which generated nearly $4 billion in revenue—the Finger Lakes region had 119 wineries, with new winery permit applications in the pipeline. The national and international press regularly reports on the region's signature wine, Riesling. At both national and international competitions, the region's wines take home more and more awards. To keep up with developments in wine, information provided by the New York Wine and Grape Foundation website is invaluable, and can be found at www.newyorkwines.org.

The Pot Still

Among the most exciting developments of the Finger Lakes bounty movement is the rebirth of two local industries that once thrived in the region but have been missing for generations—beer and spirits.

To make wine, beer, or distilled spirits, fruits and grains are the common source of fermentable sugar. The Finger Lakes region is abundant in each, and as Guy McMasters discovered in the early days of developing trade in the Pleasant Valley area south of Keuka Lake, it was more profitable to use the area's grain production as a base for spirits than to process, package, and ship it as either perishable raw grain or perishable flour. In the third US census, taken in 1810, more than fourteen thousand distillers were counted. McMaster's distillery was one of 591 in New York; fifteen years later, the number of distilleries in the state had increased to 1,129. By the census of 1830, as the temperance movement formed, the number of distilleries across the country was decreasing. In New York State, however, the vast grain fields and fruits of the western and central regions, plus the fruits of the Hudson Valley, supplied about a thousand small, local distilleries, many of which lasted until the first ban on distilled spirits went into effect in 1917, followed by Prohibition in 1920.

Making Beer and Spirits: Malting and Mashing

To malt, harvested rye, barley, wheat, oats, or corn are dried and then moistened to promote germination. Partially germinated seeds are toasted and ground.

To mash, the malted grains go into a "mash tub." Hot water is added under controlled temperature to break down the starches of the grains into fermentable sugar.

Making Beer Simplified

The mash is boiled with added hops for flavoring and stability. The mix is allowed to cool to room temperature; then yeast is added to the mash and allowed to ferment the sugar into alcohol (adding sugar increases the potential alcohol). The flavor of beer can be naturally produced from the malt toast and hops, or it can be enhanced with additions of herbs, fruits, or spices.

Making Spirits Simplified

Yeast, additional sugar, and water are added to the mash and calculated so that after fermentation the alcohol in the liquid is as high as it can be before the yeast cells die off—between 14 and 15 percent by volume.

Alcohol has a lower boiling point than water. Distilling is the process of boiling the fermented liquid so that the alcohol evaporates into the steam before the water. The steam that is captured is condensed liquid, now with a higher alcohol by volume than the liquid that was boiled. Subsequent boiling and steam capturing continues to condense the liquid until it reaches the volume of alcohol desired for the spirit being produced.

Proofing Simplified

In the eighteenth century, British sailors received rum rations. To make sure the rum had not been watered down by the supplier, naval officers "proofed" it: They doused it with gunpowder. Gunpowder floating in the rum would not burn if the rum contained less than 57.15 percent alcohol by volume. If the gunpowder did not ignite, the rum was "under proof." If the gunpowder did ignite, the rum was considered to contain the requisite alcohol and was classified "100 degrees proof." From the equation, pure alcohol is 175 (degrees) proof—at 80 proof, a spirit contains 45.72 percent alcohol by volume.

The eighty-plus-year legacy of Prohibition on local, small distilling in the state was addressed when New York laws began to loosen in 2002; then, in 2007, mimicking what had taken place in the wine industry almost exactly thirty years earlier, the legislature crafted the New York Farm Distillery Act. As the Farm Winery Act before it had done, the new distillery act reduced the financial burden on those who would start up a distillery, provided at least half the raw material—grains and

fruits—came from New York farms. One similarity between a farm winery and a farm distillery that made all the difference is that the 2007
law for the first time allowed small distillers to open a legal tasting
room and to sell their spirits at retail from the distillery.

Grappa

In the Middle Ages, under the feudal system most wealthy landowner nobles controlled
vineyards that they leased to their peasant subjects. In turn for working the vineyards and
the vintage, the lords allowed their tenant peasants to keep a small portion of the wine. The
nobles had no need for the residue of the vintage's grape crush, comprising the seeds and
the skin pulp collectively known today as "the must," which in fifteenth-century northern
Italy was called *graspe*. The peasants poured water and sweetener over the discarded *graspe*
to start another fermentation. The fermented *graspe* was further processed—distilled—to produce what we refer to as grappa.

Since the Farm Distillery Act, more than thirty craft distilleries have
started up in New York, a number that grows with each passing year.
Many of the new distilleries explore New York's spirits heritage using
heirloom grain varieties as well as local fruits to make brandies; others are creating spirits never before produced in the state. The dozen
or so distilleries that made their home in the Finger Lakes and the
overall Central New York regions in 2013 are no exception; from them
come products like whiskey produced from a blend of locally grown
corn, spelt, and malted wheat; whiskey from locally grown rye; vodka
produced from the honey of local bees; grappa made from the pulp
of locally grown and crushed Riesling grapes; and brandy from local
grapes, stone fruits, or bush berries. In keeping with the new law, these
products are all available at the distilleries. In keeping with the locavore
movement, these distilled products are found in restaurants and retail
spirits shops throughout the Finger Lakes—and beyond.

Finger Lakes Distilling

Always interested in distilling, Elmira, New York–born Brian McKenzie,
a Cornell graduate and former banker, attended a craft distiller's conference in 2007; there he met Thomas McKenzie (no relation). Thomas was
a winemaker, brewer, and distiller from Monroeville, Alabama, where
distilling was a way of life. Within days, the two formed a partnership
and were on their way toward establishing a craft distillery.

Reasoning that his home region hosted quite a number of small farms, from which they could get corn, rye, barley, and other grains, not to mention fruit from orchards and vineyards, Brian suggested they start their business in the Finger Lakes region; they would call it Finger Lakes Distillery.

The challenge to be the first Finger Lakes distillery since Prohibition made their project all the more exciting. To that end, Brian worked through the New York State Farm Bureau to draft a farm distilling bill similar to the Farm Winery Act; then he worked to petition the Albany legislature. Still, after legislation was passed in 2007 to lower the financial burden and to make it easier to establish a distillery, Finger Lakes Distilling became not the first but the second farm distillery in the state. Notwithstanding new legislation, the McKenzies were slowed by having to satisfy New York laws that force a business to invest a great deal of capital in securing land, buildings, and equipment before applying for an alcohol production license. After their application went in, they waited twelve months for a distilling permit to arrive.

From a Scottish-style whiskey distillery situated amid dozens of wineries on the east shore of Seneca Lake, Finger Lakes Distilling began with 350 gallons of pot still spirits, producing about two barrels of whiskey in each fifteen-hour day. Today, the company applies continuous distillation methods to produce between seven and eight barrels per day. Its whiskey, gin, vodka, brandy, grappa, and liqueurs are aged an average of three to four years before release. And in the spirit of lessening the impact that industry can make on the environment, the McKenzies waste nothing. Their building and tasting bar was built from reclaimed planks and wood from barns and other old buildings; grains spent after fermentation are sent to local farmers to use as animal feed.

The Return of Hops

A prominent hop-grower describes it as being simply the spirit of Wall Street carried afield.

—*New York Sun,* 1889

In 1889, Central New York was the most important hops region in the country. Breweries dotted the 125-mile stretch east from Monroe to Madison County, where most of the hops were grown.

In a Rochester Public Library historical periodical of 1992, historian Ruth Rosenberg-Napersteck named the Aqueduct Spring Brewery of 1819 as the first brewery in Rochester, fifteen years before the city's official charter of 1834. More breweries followed. Between 1819 and the eve of Prohibition, Rochester was home to about fifty breweries, many founded by German immigrants with names like Rau, Reisky, and Spies, in a string of partnerships—Rau & Reisky Brewery, Reisky & Spies Brewery—that led in 1878 to the now venerable Genesee Brewery (now the Genesee Brewing Company).

The first known brewery in the Syracuse area was established twenty-one years before that city was incorporated in 1825. The proprietor was a German immigrant and doctor named Johann Mang. After Mang, Brits and Scots dominated Syracuse breweries with names like Kellogg and Morey, 1824, and Greenway Brewery, 1858. By 1845, with over a hundred breweries listed commercially in the state, Syracuse had seven. By 1870, German immigrants—Haberle, Oesterle, and Rominger—had moved into the Syracuse brewing business and helped to make brewing the city's second largest industry, behind salt.

Francis Xavier Matt immigrated to the United States in 1880 from Baden. He worked at the Charles Bierbauer Brewery in Utica, which later became the West End Brewing Company and later still was named Matt Brewing Company. Matt shared Utica brewing history with Fort Schuyler Brewing Company, which later became the Utica Brewing Company, which wound up with the whole of that city's brewing industry.

In every case, the Erie Canal played an important role in the rise of breweries, providing water to some and shipping transportation to all. Still, at that time, beer was perishable and so the industry's strength was largely local. In the late nineteenth century, Western and Central New York breweries employed a couple of thousand people, not to mention the hundreds of hops farm families and other vendors. Soon, the development of pasteurization and the railroad opened beer traffic in the region to large breweries from outside Central New York. When the larger breweries threatened the survival of the locals, consolidation of the original Central New York breweries began.

Within a dozen years after the *New York Sun* published the quote concerning hops that opens this section, hops grown in the Pacific Northwest began to threaten New York's hops dominance. Worse was a bewildering infestation of aphids and the mildew-causing fungus *Sphaerotheca humuli*, which started the New York hops industry on its way to oblivion as more and more acreage fell to the pests at the turn of the century. Prohibition delivered the final blow in 1920. Although a number of New York breweries managed to survive the thirteen years until Repeal by producing soft drinks, hops farming had one purpose and that purpose was no more. Central New York hops were gone.

The disappearance of Central New York hops was largely responsible for the post-Prohibition change in beer flavor, as brewers after Repeal replaced hops and barley with the cheaper and more available rice and corn. Repeal also brought tight legal controls, ostensibly to protect the consumer but with the real-world effect of establishing and protecting monopolistic distribution companies. As it had done to wine and spirits, post-Prohibition regulations stifled small-scale brewing.

As in the other alcohol industries, becoming a brewer in New York after Prohibition was expensive and subject to onerous sales and distribution restrictions. Some of the restrictions were loosened in the 1990s to allow microbreweries and brewpubs to serve small-batch brewed beers on premise. Soon, microbreweries started to make their home in the Finger Lakes, in Rochester, Syracuse, Corning, Ithaca, and other locations, including inside one of the wineries along the Seneca Wine Trail. The loosening regulations left in place some fees and restrictions on distribution that many breweries wanted dismantled.

In 2000, a group of aficionados gathered, concerned that Central New York's hops-growing legacy was likely to vanish if the few remaining hops barns still standing from the past were not preserved. A year later, out of that group came the Northeast Hops Alliance with the goal to "Secure financial, scientific and community resources to support the commercial viability of commercial hops production in New York and the Northeast . . . To enhance the cultural heritage of hops production through education, agri-tourism, and architectural preservation."

Through a grant from the New York Department of Agriculture and Markets, the alliance brought in the first Cornell Agricultural Extension hops specialist in the state, based in Madison County. For many years, the alliance had no more than ten members, until the extension service and the membership organized their first hop-farming workshop in 2011. In 2013, membership had grown to around one hundred, including hops farmers throughout the entire Northeast.

As interest in microbrewing grew in Central New York, many brewers began to plant their own hops. The trend is reminiscent of small winery development in the Finger Lakes. In fact, brewers wanted what the wineries had: loosened licensing fees and better access to markets. They wanted to be farm breweries. In January 2013, Governor Andrew Cuomo signed the Farm Brewery Law, modeled after the Farm Winery Act of 1976 and the Farm Distillery Act of 2007.

To be a farm brewery, 20 percent of the ingredients to produce beer must be sourced from New York farms; that includes barley, wheat, hops, and even yeast. In expectation that the sixty acres of hops and hundred acres of barley in New York in 2013 will increase, the 20 percent rule increases over the years until, in ten years, it tops at 90 percent. The law is expected to produce growth from the few dozen breweries that exist in the state today to as many as two hundred over the next decade, an expectation that is also based on the way farm wineries developed in the state. Just like wineries and distilleries, farm breweries can pour beer for consumers on premise, in their tasting rooms, and they can sell packaged beer directly to consumers.

The real excitement behind the Farm Brewery Law is what it is expected to do for hops and barley farming in Central and Western New York. When demand for European grape varieties increased with every new farm winery that opened its doors over the past three decades, so, too, did vineyard planting as well as grapevine research and promotional budgets from the state. Everyone connected to the brewing industry believes that barley and hops farms are likely to take a similar path and increase exponentially from their current acreage, especially with help from the Cornell Agricultural Extension Service and the Department of Agriculture and Markets; the latter has already produced a video on the taste.ny.gov website to highlight the hops trend in the state.

A continuing flow into the Finger Lakes region of passionate brewers making themselves into intrepid entrepreneurs will maintain the trend until, perhaps, Central New York is again the hops (and brewing) center of the United States.

If that happens it will be an exciting addition to the fascinating story of the Finger Lakes' timeless bounty.

152   Farmland in the Finger Lakes region.
Photo courtesy Chris Houston..

Cooking with the Finger Lakes' Bounty

IN 2013, NEW YORK was the third largest milk-producing state as well as the fourth largest cheese-producing state in the country. The state ranked second in the nation in apples, which happened to be the state's largest fruit crop. New York wine production was second in the nation, and the state was second in maple syrup and cabbage; it was third in overall grape production, fourth in tart cherries, pears, sweet corn, and pumpkins, and poised to become the center of US hops production once again. Much of the production of these important farm products occurs in the central and western parts of New York. In other words, the product line in regions like the Finger Lakes has been consistent almost from the birth of local civilization.

With centuries behind them, many farm products are married to the region's topography and climate. Together, they create a cornucopia of bounty that sustains the land and the region's population. What better way to end this story than with a sampling of recipes that have been handed down and created by those who work the land and produce its products? Each of the few recipes that follow centers on the produce, livestock, and manufactured products of the Finger Lakes region of New York State. We begin with the beginning . . .

Three Sisters Stew

Courtesy of the Manataka American Indian Council

Ingredients

1 tablespoon olive or canola oil

1 jalapeño pepper, finely chopped

1 large local onion, sliced

1 clove local garlic, crushed

4 cups Finger Lakes yellow summer squash, sliced (about 1 pound)

4 cups Finger Lakes zucchini, cut into 1-inch pieces (about 2 medium)

4 cups Finger Lakes butternut squash, peeled and cubed (about 1 large)

3 cups Finger Lakes green beans, cut into 1-inch pieces (about 1 pound)

1 cup whole-kernel Finger Lakes corn

1 teaspoon dried thyme leaves

32 oz fresh dried Finger Lakes kidney or pinto beans, soaked overnight and simmered until tender

Directions

1. Heat the oil in a Dutch oven over medium heat.

2. Cook the onion, garlic, and jalapeño in oil for about 2 minutes, stirring occasionally, until the onion is tender.

3. Stir in the remaining ingredients, and cook over low heat for 10 to 15 minutes, stirring frequently, until the squash is tender.

Serves 6

Roasted Garlic, Pickled Pepper, and Corn Soup

Courtesy of Knapp Winery and Vineyard Restaurant, executive chef John McNabb

Ingredients

2 tablespoons Finger Lakes pumpkin seed oil

½ medium-sweet local onion, diced

30 cloves local garlic

1 cup roasted local red sweet peppers, cut into strips

1 cup Knapp Pasta White wine

5 pickled jalapeño peppers, chopped

4 ears Finger Lakes–grown sweet corn kernels

1 ½ teaspoons Finger Lakes grapevine-smoked salt

1 ½ quarts Finger Lakes heavy cream

3 tablespoons finely chopped local chives

1 cup Finger Lakes Parmesan kefir

New York sour cream

Directions

1. In a large saucepot, over medium-high heat, heat the oil. Add the diced onion and sauté until translucent and fragrant. Add the garlic and stir in the roasted pepper strips.

2. Deglaze the pan with Pasta White wine and bring to a simmer, stirring frequently. Add the pickled jalapeños, sweet corn, smoked salt, heavy cream, and chives to the pot; bring to a slow simmer.

3. Once the mixture is simmering, use an immersion blender to slowly pulse and puree the soup to a smooth consistency. Bring to a boil and, with the immersion blender, add the Parmesan cheese. The soup will start to thicken.

4. Simmer for 2 to 3 minutes. Stir the bottom of the pot frequently to prevent the soup from scorching throughout preparation. Enjoy topped with sour cream.

Serves 4

This soup pairs well with Knapp's Pasta White, Seyval Blanc, or Sangiovese wine.

Potato and Leek Soup with Lime Crème Fraîche and Crispy Bacon Infused with Glenora Barrel Fermented Chardonnay

Courtesy of Veraisons Restaurant at Glenora Wine Cellars, executive chef Orlando Rodriguez

Ingredients

1 local onion

5 local leeks

2 Finger Lakes celery stalks

4 tablespoons unsalted butter

½ bunch local parsley

8 Finger Lakes potatoes

1 cup Glenora Barrel Fermented
    Chardonnay

2 quarts chicken stock

1 cup heavy cream

Salt and white pepper

1 pound sliced Finger Lakes bacon

1 cup crème fraîche

1 lime

Directions

Soup

1. Sweat (gently cook) the onion, leeks, and celery in the butter. Add the parsley and sweat for approximately 5 more minutes.

2. Add the potatoes, Chardonnay, and chicken stock; simmer for approximately 30 minutes or until the potatoes are soft.

3. Blend the soup in a blender. Finish with heavy cream and season with salt and white pepper

Bacon

4. Place the bacon on a sheet pan and cook in 350°F oven for 15 minutes or until crispy.

5. Rough chop the bacon and sprinkle it over the soup.

Crème Fraîche

6. Put the crème fraîche in a bowl; juice and zest the lime into the bowl.

7. Season with salt and pepper and mix. Spoon this mixture over the soup.

Serves 10

This soup is great with a glass of Glenora Barrel Fermented Chardonnay.

Crème Brûlée Three-Cheese Fondue

Courtesy of Our Heritage Cafe at the Holiday Inn, Waterloo
(member of the Finger Lakes Cheese Trail)

Ingredients

½ cup Finger Lakes Riesling Ice Wine

¼ cup Finger Lakes Apricot Stomp Fruit Nectar

1 pound Finger Lakes chèvre cheese

1 pound Finger Lakes–produced Brie cheese, with or without rind

1 pound Finger Lakes Colby cheese, shredded

1 tablespoon Finger Lakes maple syrup

1 tablespoon Finger Lakes honey

1 tablespoon caramel

1 teaspoon pure vanilla extract

Finger Lakes culinary flake salt

Directions

1. In a medium saucepan, combine the ice wine and fruit nectar. Cook down to reduce by a quarter. Add the chèvre (the softest cheese) and stir gently with a whisk, mixing completely. Do the same with the Brie, followed by the Colby.

2. Fold in the maple syrup, honey, caramel, and vanilla.

3. Stir gently over very low heat for 5 minutes to allow the flavors to develop. If the fondue is too thick, add more ice wine; if it's too thin, add equal amounts of cheeses. Finish to taste with salt.

Serves 6–8

Pork Chop with Polenta Cake, Braised Red Cabbage, and Bourbon Pork Jus

Courtesy of the Wine and Culinary Center, Canandaigua, executive chef Michael Sokolski

Ingredients

4 sautéed Finger Lakes–raised pork chops, bone in

Polenta Cake

2 quarts water

1 quart Finger Lakes cornmeal

Salt and pepper

1 cup Finger Lakes Parmesan goat cheese, grated

½ cup Finger Lakes squash or pumpkin seed oil

Braised Red Cabbage

1 large local white onion, diced

1 head local red cabbage

1 cup Finger Lakes honey

2 cups Finger Lakes dry red wine

2 cups Finger Lakes red wine vinegar

Salt and pepper

Bourbon Pork Jus

2 local carrots, chopped

2 local onions, chopped

2 local celery stalks, chopped

2 cups Finger Lakes bourbon

2 quarts pork stock

8 ounces tomato paste

2 cups roux (mix 1 cup local bacon fat and 1 cup local flour)

Directions

1. Bring the water to a boil. Add the cornmeal and cook for 20 minutes. Finish with oil and cheese. Season to taste. Spread on a sheet tray to cool.

2. Cut the polenta into circles and in half. Fry until golden brown.

Braised red cabbage

3. Cook the onion and cabbage in a rondo (round stock pan). Add the honey, wine, and vinegar; cook until tender. Season with salt and pepper.

Bourbon pork jus

4. In a rondo (round stock pan), sauté the carrots, onions, and celery. Add the tomato paste and cook for 5 minutes. Add the alcohol and reduce by half. Add the stock and boil to reduce by half. Thicken with roux.

5. Divide the pork chops among four plates and surround with polenta and braised cabbage; top with jus.

Serves 4

Water Buffalo Sliders

Courtesy of Knapp Winery and Vineyard Restaurant, executive chef John McNabb

Ingredients

1 pound ground Finger Lakes–raised water buffalo

1 ¼ teaspoons ground herbes de Provence (savory, fennel, basil, thyme, and lavender)

5 cloves locally grown German red garlic, pressed

2 tablespoons Finger Lakes butternut squash seed oil

1 medium local sweet onion, thinly sliced

6 ounces Finger Lakes ginger tart cherry juice

6 ounces Finger Lakes smoked cheddar, sliced

¼ cup mayonnaise

8 slider rolls

4 ounces Finger Lakes–grown baby arugula leaves

1 ½ teaspoons Finger Lakes grapevine–smoked salt

Directions

1. In a medium mixing bowl, mix the ground meat, herbes de Provence, and pressed garlic until thoroughly incorporated. Portion into eight, 2-ounce patties.

2. Turn the grill onto a medium-high flame.

3. In a medium sauté pan over high heat, add the squash seed oil. Once the oil is heated, add the onion. Sauté for 2 to 3 minutes until the onion starts to caramelize. Deglaze with ginger cherry juice, reduce the heat to a simmer, and let cook for 6 to 8 minutes. The onion will start to retain the color and flavor of the juice. Turn off the heat and let the mixture cool. Strain the onion, and reserve the juice. Set aside.

4. Grill the 2-ounce patties to your preferred doneness and top with the smoked cheddar slices. Take off heat and set aside for assembly.

5. In a small mixing bowl, add the mayonnaise and whip in some of the reserved juice to form a light sauce for the finished sliders.

Assembly

6. Cut the slider rolls in half. Layer some baby arugula on the bottom of the roll, place a mini burger on top of the arugula, top the burger with some caramelized onions, sprinkle with a pinch of grapevine-smoked salt, smear the top of the bun with ginger cherry mayonnaise, and close the burger roll. Keep in place with a toothpick.

Serves 4

Pairs well with Knapp Winery Sangiovese, Cabernet Franc, or Dry Gewürztraminer.

Potatoes Au Gratin Across the Pond

Courtesy of Keeley McGarr, Keeley's Cheese Co.

Ingredients

1 pound Finger Lakes potatoes

5 ounces Keeley's Across the Pond cheese, rind removed, diced

¼ cup heavy cream

5 ounces milk

½ teaspoon freshly grated nutmeg

Salt and ground pepper to taste

2 tablespoons snipped fresh chives or chopped fresh parsley

Directions

1. Peel the potatoes and slice them about ⅛ inch thick. Fill a large pot with water and boil the potatoes.

2. Preheat the broiler.

3. Drain the potatoes and put them in a 9 x 9-inch glass baking dish.

4. Add the cheese, cream, and milk to a saucepan; mix in the nutmeg, salt, and pepper. Heat gently until all the ingredients are combined, being careful not to let the mixture come to a boil.

5. Add the saucepan ingredients to the potatoes in the baking dish and put it under the broiler on a middle rack for 5 minutes, or until browned. Garnish before serving with chives or parsley.

Serves 4

Beer-Braised Short Ribs

Courtesy of Keuka Brewing Company, Keuka Lake

Ingredients

6 pounds locally farmed short ribs

1 package dried onion soup mix

3 local onions, thinly sliced

12 ounces Keuka Brewing Bluff Point Brown Ale

2 local celery ribs, chopped

1 cup ketchup (or chili sauce)

½ cup water

Directions

1. Preheat oven to 325°F.

2. Place the ribs in a large Dutch oven. Combine the remaining ingredients and pour over the ribs. Cover the pot and bake for 3 hours or until the meat is very tender. The fat can easily be removed by refrigerating until it congeals.

Note: Instead of short ribs, you can prepare a 4- to 5-pound beef brisket or chuck roast in the same manner; cook for up to 4 hours.

Serves 8. Pairs well with Keuka Brewing Bluff Point Brown Ale.

Poached Chicken Breast in Wine and Apples

Courtesy NY Apple Country

Ingredients

6 boneless, skinless Finger Lakes chicken breasts

1 teaspoon crumbled thyme leaves

Salt and pepper to taste

½ cup Finger Lakes semi-dry white wine

1 tablespoon olive oil

2 cloves local garlic, chopped

1 cup applesauce (recipe follows)

Directions

1. Pound the chicken breasts and place them in a bowl; sprinkle evenly with the thyme and with salt and pepper to taste. Pour the wine over it all.

2. Cover and refrigerate for half an hour.

3. Put the olive oil in a skillet on high heat and sauté the garlic until slightly browned. Add the chicken breasts to the skillet, reserving the wine; sear the breasts on each side.

4. Reduce the heat to medium, pour in the wine and applesauce, cover, and simmer for about 15 minutes.

5. Adjust the salt and pepper to taste. Serve with greens and bread.

Serves 6

Applesauce

Ingredients

1 each medium McIntosh, Crispin, and Jonagold (or Cortland) apples cut into ¾-inch pieces

½ cup water

⅛ cup turbinado sugar

1 tablespoon fresh lemon juice

¼ teaspoon ground cinnamon

Directions

1. Combine the apples, water, and sugar in a saucepan; bring to a boil. Reduce the heat to low, cover, and simmer until the apples are very tender and their skins are softened, about 40 minutes.

2. Uncover and simmer until almost all the liquid has evaporated. Remove the pan from the heat; stir in the lemon juice and cinnamon.

3. Cool for 30 minutes.

4. With a fork or potato masher, mash the apple mixture until it's coarse and chunky.

Makes about 1 ½ cups

Pork Chops with Caramelized Apples

Courtesy NY Apple Country

Ingredients

4 Finger Lakes pork chops, each 1 ½ inches thick

2 teaspoons crushed dried thyme

6 tablespoon butter

4 large New York Empire or Cortland apples, cored, peeled, and cut into wedges

Vegetable oil

½ teaspoon salt

1 ½ teaspoons ground black pepper

¾ cup sugar

Directions

1. Pat the chops dry. In a small bowl mix together the thyme, pepper, and salt; season both sides of the chops and set them aside.

2. In a large, heavy skillet, melt the butter with the sugar over moderately high heat; add the apples and sauté for 30–40 minutes, until the apples begin to brown. Turn the apples and cook for 5 minutes more, until they are golden brown and the sauce is thickened. Remove from heat and keep warm.

3. Heat another heavy skillet over medium-high heat, brushing it with a little vegetable oil. Add the chops and brown on one side for about 4 minutes; turn and brown the other side for about 4 minutes then turn the chops regularly for the next 10 to 12 minutes (seek an internal temperature of 155°F).

4. Serve the chops with apples over them.

Serves 4

Seared and Roasted Pork Loin with Red Onion & Smoked Bacon Glaze

Courtesy Fox Run Vineyards, Chef Brud Holland.

Ingredients

4–6 ozs. Autumns Harvest Farm (Romulus) pork loin medallions (about 3" in diameter, 2" thick)

Black pepper, fresh ground

1 tablespoon Regional Pantry (Binghamton) sunflower oil

1 tablespoon Sunrise Farms Butter (Catskill) salted butter

1 large Remembrance Farm (Trumansburg) red onion, sliced thin

1 clove The Good Life Farm (Interlaken) garlic, sliced thin

1 tablespoon sugar

½ cup Autumns Harvest Farm thick cut, hickory smoked bacon, diced

¼ cup verjus (Verjooz; Finger Lakes Foods-Hector)

2 tablespoons Fox Run Vineyards red wine (pinot noir or cabernet franc)

Kosher salt

Fresh rosemary

Directions

1. Season the pork medallions with salt, pepper and a very light dusting of rosemary....very light. Looking for subtle.

2. In large skillet, sear the outside of each medallion until it is golden brown. Reserve on an oven proof baking dish or small roasting pan.

3. In another skillet on medium heat, allow the butter to melt, then add the onion, garlic, sugar, bacon and verjus and cook until the onions are soft stirring occasionally to keep the onions from browning.

4. Remove from the heat and add the red wine.

5. To serve, heat the pork medallions in a 400°F oven for 6-8 minutes or until the meat reaches 140°F. Place the medallions on a warm plates, spoon the onion & bacon mixture over the top and garnish with fresh leaf parsley.

Serves 4

Pairs with Fox Run Pinot Noir or Cabernet Franc.

Kale Salad with Herbed Vinaigrette

Courtesy of Samantha Buyskes, culinary chef and ambassador to the Finger Lakes food movement

Kale grows beautifully in the cool Finger Lakes climate, and with a proliferation of greenhouses and hoop houses, it is available in the region just about year-round.

Ingredients

The Salad

2 bunches locally grown kale

1 local white onion, sliced thin

4 vine-ripened local tomatoes cut into chunks

2 cups croutons (toasted with sunflower oil, salt and pepper)

The Vinaigrette

6 tablespoons locally produced sunflower oil

½ cup verjus (locally produced juice from immature grapes)

¼ cup Finger Lakes honey

2 tablespoons locally produced whole-grain mustard

1 tablespoon chopped herbs (assortment from the garden: sage, thyme, parsley)

2 cloves local garlic, smashed

Salt and pepper to taste

Directions

Whisk all of the vinaigrette ingredients together and toss with the salad.

Serves 4

Parmesan Rosemary Crackers

Courtesy of Carmella Hoffman, Sunset View Creamery

Ingredients

1 cup all-purpose Finger Lakes flour

½ teaspoon salt

½ cup finely grated Sunset View Creamery Heritage Cheese

1 teaspoon rosemary leaves

¼ cup unsalted butter

¼ cup cream or half-and-half

Coarse salt, pepper, and sesame or poppy seeds for sprinkling

Directions

1. Preheat the oven to 400°F. Line a baking sheet with parchment paper (or lightly dust it with flour)

2. Put flour, salt, cheese rosemary, and butter in a food processor or mixing bowl; pulse until butter and flour are combined.

3. Add the cream or half-and-half, and mix or process until a dough forms. (If necessary, you can add more cream a teaspoon at a time until the dough comes together but isn't sticky.)

4. Roll out dough on a floured surface until it's ¼ inch thick or less, adding flour as needed. Poke the dough all over with a fork and sprinkle it with salt, pepper, and seeds.

5. Cut into 1 ½-inch squares and place on the baking sheet about ½ inch apart.

6. Bake until moderately brown, about 12 minutes.

7. Cool on rack and store in a tin.

Makes about 30 crackers

Maple-Apple Upside Down Cake

Courtesy of Veraisons Restaurant at Glenora Wine Cellars, executive chef Orlando Rodriguez

Ingredients

1 cup Finger Lakes maple syrup

3 Finger Lakes–grown apples, peeled, cored, and cut into eighths

2 cups all-purpose Finger Lakes flour

1 teaspoon baking powder	1 teaspoon baking soda
1 teaspoon Finger Lakes salt	3 Finger Lakes eggs
1 cup buttermilk	1 teaspoon vanilla extract
6 ounces unsalted butter, softened	1 ⅓ cups sugar

Directions

1. Preheat the oven 325°F. Butter and flour a 10-inch cake pan.

2. In a large saucepan, bring the maple syrup to a boil over high heat, then simmer over low heat until very thick and reduced to ½ cup, about 20 minutes. Pour the thickened syrup into the cake pan. Arrange the apples in the pan in two concentric circles, overlapping them slightly.

3. In a bowl, whisk the flour, baking powder, baking soda, and salt. In a measuring cup, whisk the eggs with the buttermilk and vanilla. In the bowl of a stand-up mixer fitted with a paddle, beat the butter and sugar at medium speed until fluffy, about 3 minutes.

4. Beat the dry and wet ingredients into the mixer bowl in three alternating batches until the batter is smooth, scraping down the sides of the bowl.

5. Scrape the batter over the apples and spread it in an even layer. Bake for 45 minutes, until it's golden on top and a toothpick inserted in the center comes out clean. Let cool for 45 minutes.

Makes one 10-inch cake. Serve with Glenora Port.

Pumpkin Pie

Courtesy of the Manataka American Indian Council

Ingredients

½ cup packed dark brown sugar

1 teaspoon ground cinnamon

1 teaspoon ground ginger

¼ teaspoon ground nutmeg

Pinch of ground cloves

16 ounces pumpkin puree (fresh Finger Lakes pumpkin, of course)

1 ¼ cups evaporated skim milk

3 large egg whites

9-inch unbaked pie shell (or use your favorite recipe for 9-inch single-crust basic pie pastry from Finger Lakes flour)

Directions

1. Preheat the oven to 450°F.

2. In a large bowl, beat all the filling ingredients until no lumps remain. Pour into the pie shell.

3. Bake for 10 minutes; reduce the heat to 325°F and bake for 50 minutes more, or until a knife inserted in the center comes out clean.

Note: To avoid overbrowning of the piecrust's fluted edge, cover it with narrow strips of aluminum foil. Remove the foil during the last 15 minutes of baking.

Serves 8

Buckwheat Walnut Bars

Courtesy of Hunt Country Vineyards, Keuka Lake

Ingredients

Crust

⅔ cup confectioner's sugar

1 ½ cups unbleached white flour

½ cup buckwheat flour

½ teaspoon salt

½ teaspoon ground cinnamon

1 cup butter (2 sticks)

Topping

½ cup butter (1 stick)

1 teaspoon vanilla

½ teaspoon ground cinnamon

½ cup buckwheat honey

½ cup cream or milk

½ cup packed brown sugar

3 cup walnuts, coarsely chopped

Directions

Crust

1. Grease a 9 x 12-inch baking pan with butter. Preheat the oven to 350°F.

2. Mix the confectioner's sugar, white flour, buckwheat flour, salt, and cinnamon.

3. Cut the butter into the mixture with a fork or pastry blender and mix until fine crumbs form.

4. Pat the crust into the baking pan.

5. Bake for 20 minutes; then, remove from the oven, but keep the oven burning.

Topping

6. Melt the butter over low heat—don't burn it. Mix in the remaining ingredients, and spread it all over the crust.

7. Put the pie in the oven and bake for 25 to 30 minutes.

8. Cool completely.

Makes 36 squares

Pair with Hunt Country Vidal Blanc Ice Wine or Late Harvest Vignoles.

BIBLIOGRAPHY

Champlin, Charles, and Ray Bradbury. *Back There Where the Past Was: A Small Town Boyhood.* Syracuse, NY: Syracuse University Press, 1989.

Chapman, Paul Jones, and Edward Hadley Glass. *The First 100 Years of the New York State Agricultural Experiment Station at Geneva New York.* Ithaca, NY: Cornell University, 1999.

Cutter, William Richard, editor. *Genealogical and Family History of Central New York, Volume 1.* New York: Lewis Historical Publishing, 1911.

Dawson, Evan. *Summer in a Glass: The Coming of Age of Winemaking in the Finger Lakes.* New York: Sterling Publishing, 2011.

Eckles, C.H., and G.F. Warren. *Dairy Farming.* New York: Macmillan, 1916.

Fippin, Elmer Otterbein. *Rural New York.* New York: Macmillan, 1921.

Folger, J.C., and S.M. Thomson. *The Commercial Apple Industry of North America.* New York: Macmillan, 1921.

Gabler, James. *Passions: Wines and Travels of Thomas Jefferson.* Baltimore: Bacchus Press, 1995.

Hall, Henry, editor. *America's Successful Men of Affairs: An Encyclopedia of Contemporaneous Biography, Volume 1.* New York: New York Tribune Association, 1899.

Hedrick, Ulysses Prentiss. *A History of Agriculture in the State of New York.* New York: New York State Agricultural Society, 1933.

Kerber, Jordan E., editor. *Archeology of the Iroquois: Selected Readings and Other Research Sources.* Syracuse, NY: Syracuse University Press, reprint edition 2007.

Ontario County, NY. *Courtesy VisitFingerLakes.com*

Kyvig, David. *Repealing National Prohibition*. Kent, OH: Kent State University Press, 2000.

Melone, Harry R. *History of Central New York*. Indianapolis: Historical Publishing, 1932.

McGovern, Patrick E. *Ancient Wine: The Search for the Origins of Viniculture*. Princeton, NJ: Princeton University Press, 2003.

McMaster, Guy H. *History of the Settlement of Steuben County, New York*. Bath, NY: Underhill, 1893.

New York State Historical Association Editorial Committee. *A Guide to the Empire State*. New York, 1940.

Pinney, Thomas. *A History of Wine in America, Volume 1: From the Beginnings to Prohibition*. Berkeley: University of California Press, 1989.

———. *A History of Wine in America, Volume 2: From Prohibition to the Present*. Berkeley: University of California Press, 2005.

Powers, Mabel (Yeh Sen Noh Wehs). *Stories the Iroquois Tell Their Children*. New York: American Book Company, 1917.

Ritchie, William A. *The Archeology of New York State*. Fleischmanns, NY: Purple Mountain Press, revised edition 1977.

Schlebecker, John L., and Andrew W. Hopkins. *A History of Dairy Journalism in the United States 1810–1950*. Madison: University of Wisconsin Press, 1957.

Sheldon, J.P. *Dairy Farming: The Theory, Practice and Method of Dairying*. London, New York: Cassell, Petter, Galpin, date unknown.

Sernett, Milton. *Say Cheese: The Story of the Era When New York State Cheese Was King*. Cazenovia, NY: self-published, 2012.

Sherer, Richard. *Crooked Lake and the Grape*. Self-published, ND.

Sturtevant, William C., editor. *Handbook of North American Indians, Volume 15*. Washington, DC: Smithsonian Institution, date unknown.

Taber, George M. *Judgment of Paris: California vs. France and the Historic 1976 Paris Tasting*. New York: Scribner, 2006.

Articles, Talks, Theses, Reports

American Temperance Union. Report of the Executive Committee of the American Temperance Union. New York: S. W. Benedict, 1840.

Cazentre, Don. "Finger Lakes Cheese Trail Offers One-Stop Sampling at First Cheese Fest." *Syracuse Post Standard,* July 9, 2012.

Clarke, Paul. "Still Life: New York's Distillery Boom Revives a Spirited Tradition." *Imbibe,* March–April 2012.

Cropp, Bob, and Terry Graf. *The History and Role of Dairy Cooperatives.* Ithaca, NY: Cornell University, January 2001.

Dial, Tom. "Charles Fournier Honored." *Syracuse New Times,* September 1982.

Fick, Gary W., and William J. Cox. *The Agronomy of Dairy Farming in New York State.* Ithaca, NY: Cornell University, Soil, Crop and Atmospheric Sciences, June 1995.

Goresline, Harry, and Donald K. Tressler. "Cooperative Research in Wine Making at Geneva, NY." *American Wine and Liquor Journal,* June 1937.

Martin, Bridget. *Analysis of Lakeside Deposits: Seneca Lake, Geneva, New York.* Annual Keck Symposium, Vassar College, 2005.

Memmott, Jim. "Remarkable Rochester: Craft Breweries, a Rochester Tradition." *Rochester Democrat and Chronicle*, October 29, 2013.

Mudge, Ken, Jules Janick, Steven Sofield, and Eliezer E. Goldschmidt. "A History of Grafting." *Cornell University Horticultural Reviews* 35, John Wiley and Sons, 2009.

Newman, James L. "Vines, Wine, and Regional Identity in the Finger Lakes Region." *Geographical Review* 76, American Geographical Society, July 1986.

Ourecky, David K., and G. L. Slate. *Jewel Black Raspberry.* NYS Agricultural Experiment Station at Geneva Bulletin 35, August 1973.

Rosenberg-Napersteck, Ruth. "A Brief History of Brewing in Rochester." *Rochester History,* Rochester Public Library, Spring 1992.

Tauer, Loren W., and, Krishna P. Belbase. *Technical Efficiency of New York Dairy Farms.* Ithaca, NY: Cornell University study, April 1987.

Turow, Eve. "The Distant Past and Recent Rise of New York's Brewing and Distilling Industry." *Village Voice,* June 27, 2013.

Walker, Harrison Howell. "Fruitful Shores of the Finger Lakes." *National Geographic,* May 1941.

Warren, George Frederick. *The Apple Industry of Wayne and Orleans Counties, New York.* Thesis, Cornell University, 1905.

Helpful Websites

agriculture.ny.gov (New York Department of Agriculture and Markets)

applejournal.com (New York Apple Orchards)

canandaiguawinetrail.com (Canandaigua Lake Wine Trail)

cayugawinetrail.com (Cayuga Lake Wine Trail)

ediblefingerlakes.com (*Edible Finger Lakes* magazine)

fingerlakesagriculture.com (Finger Lakes Agriculture)

fingerlakesbeertrail.com (Finger Lakes Beer Trail)

flcb.org (Finger Lakes Culinary Bounty)

flcheesetrail.com (Finger Lakes Cheese Trail)

ganondagan.org (Ganondagan Preservation)

greenstar.coop (GreenStar Cooperative, Ithaca)

keukawinetrail.com (Keuka Lake Wine Trail)

ilovenyfarms.com (Finger Lakes Farms)

ilovethefingerlakes.com (I Love the Finger Lakes)

lib.rochester.edu (River Campus Libraries, University of Rochester)

manataka.org (Manataka American Indian Council)

nativeamericannetroots.net (Native American Forum)

newyorkwines.org (New York Wine and Grape Foundation)

nyapplecountry.com (New York Apple Association)

regionalcouncils.ny.gov (New York Economic Development Council)

rocwiki.org (The People's Guide to Rochester)

rurdev.usda.gov (US Department of Agriculture, Rural Development)

seneclakewine.com (Seneca Lake Wine Trail)

whisperingbooks.com (classic fairy tales, myths, and legends from throughout the world)

INDEX